Lifting the Veil:

Raising Consciousness

CONNIE HOWELL

This is an IndieMosh book

brought to you by MoshPit Publishing
an imprint of Mosher's Business Support Pty Ltd

PO Box 147
Hazelbrook NSW 2779

indiemosh.com.au

Copyright © Connie Howell 2017

The moral right of the author has been asserted in accordance with the Copyright Amendment (Moral Rights) Act 2000.

All rights reserved. Except as permitted under the Australian Copyright Act 1968 (for example, fair dealing for the purposes of study, research, criticism or review) no part of this publication may be reproduced, stored in a retrieval system, or transmitted in any form or by any means, electronic, mechanical, photocopying, recording or otherwise, without the written permission of the publisher.

Cataloguing-in-Publication entry is available from the National Library of Australia: http://catalogue.nla.gov.au/

Title:	Lifting the Veil: Raising Consciousness
Author:	Howell, Connie (1949–)
ISBNs:	978-1-925739-21-3 (paperback)
	978-1-925739-22-0 (ebook – epub)
	978-1-925739-23-7 (ebook – mobi)

Cover design by Connie Howell and Ally Mosher

Cover layout by Ally Mosher at allymosher.com

Images from Adobe Stock

The author has made every effort to ensure that the information in this book was correct at the time of publication. However, the author and publisher accept no liability for any loss, damage or disruption incurred by the reader or any other person arising from any action taken or not taken based on the content of this book. The author recommends seeking third party advice and considering all options prior to making any decision or taking action in regard to the content of this book.

From my heart to yours

Other titles by Connie Howell:

Portable Snippets of Wisdom

Perfectly Imperfect: How to be Imperfect and Remain Lovable

Walking Between Two Worlds: From the Known to the Unknown

Foreword

Some of this material undoubtedly comes from my own unconscious mind and from my personal compendium of experiences throughout this lifetime. There are also parts that I know have come to me directly from a higher stream of consciousness. I have Spirit brothers and sisters that contribute important material for all my books via the pool of consciousness that I tap into. I can sense the difference between that energy and my own. When I am writing about my own experiences from this current earthly perspective my vibrational input is slightly different.

When I enter into those other levels of consciousness that give me access to deeper sources of awareness it comes from a finer vibrational depository that includes my higher self. This is not the same awareness that I use for going about my daily business. I access my higher wisdom when I get into the zone of writing. Therefore you can see that there are several layers of interaction that make this book complete.

Whatever form the information takes or the vibrational source of the material, it comes to me as an easy flow of words through a magnified thought process along with a greater awareness. *The others* that contribute, comically refer to themselves as the 'ghost writers'—which I find hysterically funny. They have such a fabulous sense of humour that fits so easily with my own. I have always loved having a good belly laugh. They are no longer of this earthly vibration and I feel privileged to be on their 'team'. My job is to make their stream of consciousness along with my own manifest through the written word, however unlike channelling I do not step aside to let others speak through me. I simply merge into the higher vibration for a short while. There are no names exchanged for names only satisfy the egos need to know and really, we are all one consciousness.

I view them as members of a council of enlightened souls who come to share their higher wisdom for the benefit of all those who are as yet unable to reach a high enough energetic vibration to break through the veil of illusion.

They seek no kudos and no recognition for they are beyond ego. They simply come to serve and have fun while they do it. Humour does not cease with the death of the body and I for one am most grateful for that.

They can encourage and help motivate us into not giving up when it all seems too hard. They guide us when we fall back into doubt and when we wonder if our minds are making up fantastic stories even when we have received irrefutable evidence that we are not alone.

It is up to you as to what you do with the information in this book; you may take it or leave it but if you have chosen to pick it up in the first place then there is part of you that is desperate to *know*. You are a seeker of higher truth just like me. There is an inner drive to find the essential essence of you that you feel is missing yet has been there all the time. It is just out of your conscious awareness. You simply need to remember. Like them I need nothing from you, I am simply playing my part in offering you the information. Whether you run with it or toss it aside is your call.

As I write I know that the content isn't just for you, I continuously learn from it too and marvel at some of my own instinctual remembering and depth of knowing. Along with my friends in spirit who so lovingly share from that higher perspective, I love the service of it all.

I am on a journey just as you are and hopefully if I am a step ahead I can turn and call you forward knowing that it is at times a difficult path. The temptation to give up when feeling alone can be overwhelming. I can only say that I understand as I have felt that way many times and I meander in and out of the enthusiasm to keep on keeping on. Sometimes it is best to rest, let go and let loose for a while then move on when the time is right and the energy is there to do so.

I encourage you to keep seeing the signs and taking the steps that call you forward into your greater awareness and magnificence. Feeling discouraged and low in energy is often part of the journey but know that it will pass in time. Make sure you rest and take care of yourselves when feeling this way. Don't fight it for it gives you the opportunity to regroup and reassess your personal passage into greatness. Everything has a reason and perfect timing far beyond the intellectual grasp so keep trusting and walking toward your greater truths.

It is with deep love that I entrust this book to you in order that you find the clues and information embedded in it especially for you. They are my humble contribution to this leg of your journey home.

Connie Howell

Contents

Foreword v
Acknowledgements x
Chapter 1 1
  What is The Veil? *1*
Chapter 2 14
  The Nature of Reality *14*
Chapter 3 27
  Earth: the great mother *27*
Chapter 4 34
  Enjoy everything, be attached to nothing *34*
Chapter 5 46
  Resistance: friend or foe? *46*
Chapter 6 55
  The Collective Nightmare *55*
Chapter 7 65
  Love as a vibration *65*
Chapter 8 77
  Learn to read the signs *77*
Chapter 9 84
  Getting Real *84*
Chapter 10 92

Lifting the Veil

The big picture	92
Chapter 11	98
Building Trust	98
Chapter 12	104
Rewrite your story	104
Chapter 13	117
Layer upon Layer	117
Chapter 14	127
Life is a journey	127
Suggested Reading	139
Useful websites	140

Connie Howell

Acknowledgements

Thank you to my best friend Jenny Richards for always taking the time to read through my work and give me encouraging feedback even though she has her own busy life. To my dear friend Jane Bevan thanks for the beautiful handmade earrings she donated for me to sell. Walter my husband always encourages me to be unique and to keep on writing. He loves knowing that I am being creative and, sharing that creativity with those who choose to read my books.

My son Jason generates interest in his circle of friends when I have a new book released which opens up the scope to reach those of his generation that otherwise might not find me. Thank you for your support Jay.

Thank you to all my friends that continue to encourage and support me.

I am deeply moved and filled with gratitude towards all of you that buy my books. Sharing information with you is one of the biggest motivations for me to continue writing. Thank you for giving them your time and attention.

I am so fortunate to have a great team in Jenny Mosher, Ally (Mosher) Taylor, Samantha Stevenson and Sarah McCloghry who between them make my manuscript into a book.

Row, row, row your boat, gently down the stream,
Merrily, merrily, merrily, merrily life is but a dream.

Eliphalet Oram Lyte

Chapter 1

What is The Veil?

Many Beings watch over us; we are not alone. Though this may be a disturbing idea for some, on the whole it is a reassuring and comforting thought for me. I think I have always believed in the possibility of other life forms and that is why programs and movies such as the *Star Trek* and *Star Wars* series appeal to me and many others. It seems perfectly reasonable to me to think of galactic councils and Beings with a higher consciousness looking out for us in a neighbourly way, although admittedly some others may not be as benevolent. Some would call me a dreamer and fantasist for thinking this but it feels plausible to me and that is all that matters. Having said that, I must clarify that I don't go gazing in the clouds looking for spaceships and I don't crave alien contact—that is not my thing. However, the idea of advanced life forms that come to help humanity appeals to me, especially as we seem to be making such a mess of things. At times we are like children fighting and squabbling about who has what and who did what to whom. We carry various streams of consciousness within us and that is why we are unique as individuals whilst also being connected to a mass consciousness.

There is a vast array of dimensions that the human mind is unaware of. That is simply because when we incarnate into physical reality we have to focus on being a physical entity. That is how we learn about the pleasures and pain of human existence and it is the reason we incarnate. That along with wanting to help the earth ascend to the next level in her development and to enhance the overall expansion of the universal consciousness. I question if we are doing a good job.

In time the soul stirs, prodding the mind. It then inevitably roams to questions of *why am I here, what is my purpose* and *who am I?* Pondering these and other questions begins the awakening process. An opening of the mind begins to allow information and knowledge to be delivered so that the consciousness expands and starts to see a wider version of reality. The picture then becomes more panoramic rather than the narrow aspect seen only from the shallow band of physical reality. The soul moves us into wanting to know and understand more than what we perceive through the five senses alone. We have an inbuilt desire to understand the greater mysteries. It may or may not be active during our present incarnation.

Limited vision brings limited understanding. Opening the mind allows us to see truths that have always been there but were previously unseen by eyes that are shielded by the blurred lenses of our perceived reality.

Commonly known as the veil, there is an invisible construct that serves to keep us focused on the five senses. It also protects us from sensory overload. When the time comes for the veil to be lifted we can then see and comprehend how limiting but necessary the veil has been up until this point. In most cases it isn't lifted until we can deal with the vastness of *what is* and have expanded our awareness sufficiently. That can take many lifetimes and when the yearning to know is great enough to start looking deeper the awakening process is activated.

It is up to us to feel the pull of the soul towards awakening to higher consciousness and to respond with gratitude and eagerness when we step out of the limited consciousness we usually operate from into unlimited and unbridled awareness. What freedom, what exhilaration to be unshackled from the heavy chains of servitude to a mindset driven by an ego that wants to keep us small and unassuming.

Primarily we are here to fully experience the human condition and to grow as a result. The veil is essential so that we can concentrate on being human. All the things that constitute being human can make us temporarily forget that we are Universal Beings, that we are one with the Universe/God/Creator. It is somewhat like suffering from amnesia. Unaware and without memory of whom we are. If the veil is lifted by our consciousness being raised high enough we can then start to see the totality of what we are. We still live a human life but we now know that it is not our true identity.

What does waking up mean? It is a process of understanding and expanding the awareness to a fuller view of the overall picture. What you think of as *mind* is only a tiny fraction of what consciousness really is and your mind is not the brain, though that is where you may experience thoughts and thinking.

Consciousness is everywhere, we dwell in consciousness and it dwells in us. There is no separation: we are part of everything and everything is a part of us.

Though each of us perceives that we have our *own* portion of consciousness—our own thoughts and ideas—we are also connected to what Carl Jung, the famous Swiss psychiatrist called the collective unconscious; the one that contains the bigger pool of thinking and thoughts. We may believe that we are separate, individual and autonomous but whose thoughts are we really thinking? Are we the generators of the trillions of thoughts that stream through the mind each and every day or do thoughts just happen? We have access to a greater consciousness that some call Oneness/God/Universe. It doesn't really matter what name you give it. However we have a tendency to believe that we are isolated from each other and that our mind is unconnected from all other minds including and especially the universal mind.

This Higher Power created everything and if you believe that, then you must also believe that nothing can be separate, that we are all related and are part of that one source that created us. We may experience ourselves as individual but it is neither our permanent nor true condition. We simply forget that we are an integral part of creation therefore connected at the deepest level. The universal consciousness is experiencing itself through us in all our various forms.

Everything contains life and consciousness at some level. It is only *humans* that assign consciousness to things that are considered to be alive and aware in the same way that we are, with a higher level of intelligence and the ability to reason. But do stones, trees, plants, mountains and rivers have a form of consciousness? Masuro Emoto the Japanese author, researcher and photographer carried out many experiments on water believing that water molecules could react to both positive and negative words. He also experimented on polluted water rendering it clean through prayer and visualisation. The photos in Masuro's books which discuss the consciousness of water molecules gives much food for thought and insight into how we can influence our own wellbeing. *The Hidden Messages in Water* is one of his more prominent books and became a bestseller. He says that because our bodies are largely made up of water that we can influence our health by visualisation and directing loving thoughts and intentions inward.

Everything has a vibration that varies in speed and density, the denser the vibration the more visible the form. As humans we judge life by what we know, what we can see and that which we find acceptable. What if other species—that do not conform to our preconceived ideas about what life forms look like—reside in other dimensions that we cannot normally see? Does that mean they do not exist? If we are blind to those other dimensions we can at best only speculate. But if you can see them whilst others cannot, does that mean that they are merely figments of a vivid imagination, the stuff of science fiction? We have a tendency to dismiss what we can't explain or understand. Much of this is done out of fear and limited thinking. There was a time in history where the idea of machines that could fly in the air or ships that could dive underwater was considered impossible. So what if there really are machines that can travel between worlds?

These are interesting questions to contemplate. They probably will lead to many more questions: this is part of the waking up process. The intelligence that created us is ever evolving and expanding and that includes our individual evolution and expansion which then contributes to the whole.

Psychic and mediumistic abilities can be steps to the

opening up of greater awareness but there is so much more and so many other ways to move forward. Enlightenment is a result of realising who we truly are but even then there is more. Enlightenment comes in many stages. It isn't a one stop shop. We never stop growing and learning. Everyone at some point will become enlightened—that is a surety and a natural part of the evolutionary process. It may not be in this lifetime or the next but it will come to all of us eventually.

One of the primary reasons for incarnating into physical reality is to know what it is like to be and live as humans with physical attributes. The loves, the laughs the pains and sorrows are all equally important. Earth is a giant school, a place of immense opportunity to learn the exquisite lessons we are offered here. Not only that, we also have the ability to *wake up* and recognise that we are divine by nature bringing Heaven to Earth. I know that the term *wake up* may be confusing for some of you so think of it in terms of suddenly having clarity about something that before you just couldn't see. Having then seen it clearly it is like a revelation or a light bulb moment.

Throughout our lifetime we find ourselves engaging with many people that act as mirrors, enabling us to see reflections of the negative and positives about ourselves. The more polished the mirror the more our true identity is revealed. It is up to us to work out which are the real images as opposed to the illusionary ones.

We are given people on both sides of the veil to help and guide us; no one is left alone to muddle through even though we may at times feel a deep sense of abandonment and aloneness, especially if life is proving difficult. We look at others who are richer and have what we lack, seemingly without any problems and we label them lucky. We may envy or resent them. Yet in the totality of all our lives we have had all kinds of experiences and lifestyles. We forget that maybe the last life was fuller, happier. *Life is neither a penance nor a reward.* All experiences lead to growth. It is a chance to evolve, to know love and compassion and grow through pain and suffering. Conversely by leading a good life we can experience gratitude that this time we are doing it sweet. All experiences are valid and of equal importance. Each brings specific lessons to bring fullness to the soul.

I have been the recipient of much kindness in my life. Sometimes I felt deserving of the help while other times it blew me away to know that people could be so kind when I had so obviously not lived up to my idea of acceptable societal standards of behaviour. Set boundaries and rules can cause us much distress as we struggle to conform to the societal guidelines of how we should live. So as humans we walk along a two-edged sword. Whichever side we fall or deliberately choose to walk, lasting peace is often illusive. We can either fit in or be seen as rebellious and non-conformist. *Such is life.*

Ups and downs come as regularly as the waves of the ocean. So how do we find the middle ground? Are we in fact meant to or is it for us to rise and fall with the rhythm of life? What is life about and what is its purpose?

Enlightened people don't become enlightened by chance, they put in the hard effort and discipline required to break through the vice-like grip of the ego and the temptation to judge themselves and others. This can be a constant battle between what is considered right or wrong by the cultures we are born into. When the higher meaning of the situations we face daily are understood we don't get so caught up in personalising the ins and outs of daily life.

Mastery comes through direct experience rather than just academia and intellectual pursuits that are so dearly prized. To experience the fullness of life is to more fully comprehend the nature and meaning of life. Modernity has provided us with great strides forward in many ways. Advances in medicine, technology, housing and transport have all brought benefits that are undeniable and yet we seem to be a more stressed world in spite of it. We have bigger and more powerful weapons and along with them a threat hangs over us, as the possibility of someone pushing the button in a fit of defiance or megalomania is ever present. The pursuit of ultimate power over others is evident in some of the world leaders who verbally push and shove each other on a regular basis. Waking up is now more necessary than ever.

In fundamental ways we have lost our connection to life itself by being caught up in busyness. We have busy lives and busy minds. Social media dominates the lives of our younger generations and many of us too. So how can we relax and connect to our higher self when we are always switched on with texting on our phones and sitting for hours at computers? There are a myriad of addictions and distractions that distance us from our true selves, cutting us off from the deeper more profound aspects of life and experiencing the inner wisdom present within us all.

In my own life a large portion of my time was filled with feelings of anxiety, fear and thoughts of the past or the future. I also worried about what people thought of me or what I thought of them. Thoughts of what ifs and of ageing and dying all crowded out 'what is' so I missed being present most of the time. I often had feelings of powerlessness and impotence which created more worry and anxiety. It becomes a vicious cycle that is hard to break free from.

I have revelled in the good times and resisted the downtimes. I have agonised about life, the purpose of being here and the concerns of not being here. I have felt all the feelings and thought all the thoughts about the right diet, the wrong diet, how to maintain health and every other kind of malady that may befall human existence. You name it I have felt it, thought it, done it or had someone close to me do it. I am sure you have too.

Such is the nature and dilemma of life. It is up to each of us to do what we can to prevent ourselves from drowning in the pool of humanity.

Spirit says, 'We don't want you to be perfect. We want you to overcome the idioms of the ego. For it is the unbridled ego that casts you into the shadows and the swinging of the pendulum between feeling either unworthy or superior and all between. If there is no balance then troubles persist'.

The middle ground is where we can find humility and the true connection to source. It is the gateway to lifting the veil. There you find that you don't believe one thing or another you simply know you are divine by nature and that you are having a human experience. You know that love is the ultimate way forward and you become one with everything, at least some of the time. When you know that you are intrinsically divine you can let loose the tight grip on human foibles and accept the *now* because you understand that everything is as it should be, in perfect order even though chaos may be present all around you. When you are in the *now* you enter into the flow of life and cease struggling.

Humans often misunderstand the reasons for being human. It is not to serve some distant deity, nor a punishment or a test to prove that you are worthy or acceptable. You are already this and more. You took human form to experience life as a human being with the totality of all that it entails.

Instead of resisting life and fighting with yourself to be better, more intellectual, more amazing or more anything, simply embrace all that life has to offer you. This includes the good, the bad and the downright scary, for it is in facing your fears that you find the strength and power of who you really are. Life is your chance to try on all the different costumes, dress up, dress down, be rich, be poor, be good or be bad. All of it is useful in the overall growth of your soul.

Imagine being an actor at the end of their life looking back at the opportunities gained by having played such a rich medley of roles. A body of work so satisfying that it nourishes the soul and is made more poignant with the knowledge that they were only roles not reality and, that the real you remains intact when all the roles are finished.

In my other books *Perfectly Imperfect: How to be Imperfect and Remain Lovable* and *Walking Between Two Worlds*, perfection and acting out roles are themes that I frequently use because we can easily relate to them. Movies are an everyday part of our lives. Spirit talks to us in the language of the day so that we can understand what they are trying to convey to us. Often meaning gets lost in the translation and we may have to sift a little to get to the core of it.

Though I advocate viewing life like watching a good movie I often forget my own advice. I fluctuate between frustration and disappointment to elation and delight about life. I still have difficulty in my attempts to master the many aspects of life so I understand and live with the struggle. Even letting go of the struggle can be a struggle!

Sometimes the merry-go-round spins so fast it is hard to jump off without getting hurt. Even though I have a good life I sometimes have trouble embracing it fully. Boredom was a constant companion and something that I fought with rather than allowing it to reveal its secrets. After all doesn't boredom mean having nothing interesting to do? Or is it indicative of a deeper form of unrest, resistance or denial?

Walking a spiritual path is often fraught with challenges and I have frequently asked myself if it is worth the effort and yet I cannot turn back. Nor do I want to. Sometimes feeling stuck is a terrible conundrum and a test of endurance and I often wonder if the spiritual icons and ancestors of the past have felt what I feel—although I am sure that they have.

The agony I know well, the ecstasy is fleeting, it comes and goes. Though many books give us insights and instruction as to the best ways to proceed I have found that though they can be helpful nothing is better than one's own inner connection to the innate guidance system. That and the experience of connecting with other dimensions are unsurpassable. I believe we are in the time of direct revelation: that it is available and achievable to all. Wishing, feeling, visualising and being positive may all be helpful tools for some of us but not for everyone. There isn't a 'one size fits all' in spiritual development, we must find our own path, the one especially set out for us by us.

Authors like me can only offer their own experience and ways of communicating which can contain helpful guidance and advice, but ultimately I believe that each of us must walk the road we are drawn to with the understanding

Connie Howell

that all roads will get you there. Some may be quicker some longer but nevertheless we will all get there in the end.

Now that's a comforting thought.

You can wake up from illusion
Start challenging your programmed beliefs and
Your forgetfulness
Begin by asking yourself the right questions
Start with
'Am I asleep, if so how do I wake up?'

Chapter 2

The Nature of Reality

Are we really here or are we being dreamed by the Universe? If we are being dreamed and we become aware of it can we change the dream by becoming lucid dreamers? Perhaps that is what co-creation is really all about. When we become cognisant of the facts of being dreamed we can lighten up and be more playful with life, why cling so desperately to our notions of reality and why judge reality as a purely physical phenomenon? These are interesting questions and I wonder if it has ever occurred to you to ask them. The five senses dominate the material world and is convincing to say the least. If you don't investigate beyond the surface then you will live within this reality without knowing that there is more.

In order to live comfortably within the confines of the physical dimension that we find ourselves in we may become arrogant in our attitudes towards other possible existences that are far beyond our intellectual understanding. There are many versions of reality because each of us perceives reality a little differently and in some cases our versions of reality are diametrically opposed. Does this mean that one person's reality is truer than the others or that certain views of reality are wrong? Believing that our interpretations of reality are right and therefore others wrong is what separates and divides us. Wanting to be right causes us to be rigid and closed off to other possibilities

Reality is not a set phenomenon, for every time we get a deeper insight and understanding of something our reality changes. It is fluid and constantly flowing if we allow it to be so—without interference.

We cling to our perceived notions of sanity for fear of *losing our minds*. If we were to allow ourselves to set adrift in the ocean of possibilities where would that take us? The thought of even considering the idea that there may be multiple dimensions of reality and a multiverse can be confusing and frightening for most of us unless we believe it is purely fictitious like in the movies.

Then we can go home and forget about it by going back to our sense of what is real. Who would want to be thought of as insane, delusional, fanciful or psychiatrically impaired by saying they actually believed otherwise? We live in tribes and so we want to fit into the society of which we are members and have the need to belong too. Thereby we usually fall into line and accept the tribal agreements of what reality is.

How is it then that some individuals are able to see into these other dimensions and interact with them and, how do they, *knowing what they know* live amongst the majority that don't? We either believe that they have a gift or that they have lost touch with reality. One gets the sense of having to justify or explain the ability to sense other realities in scientific and intellectual terms to have it accepted and not be labelled crazy. Even then we still call it into question. Why are we so afraid?

Society as a whole seems to need to maintain the bubble of sanity and rationality within the confines of how we as a whole define what being rational and sane is. We read of people in religious books that had the gift of prophecy, dream interpretation and other abilities yet we are deemed questionable if we are seen to have the same abilities.

There is a consensus of what makes physical reality normal and everything outside of these parameters is deemed abnormal. There is still a mass denial and unconsciousness which is a powerful drug in keeping all other possibilities out of range and that delegates them to the outer fringes of normality. We may have been anaesthetised into a deep sleep, unaware of other dimensions and entities; but now many are awakening.

What is the purpose of this mass perception that Earth is the only planet to support life and that we are the only beings in existence? Perhaps it is too frightening to think of alien species that may have their different eye on us and our beautiful blue home. Or maybe we were meant to forget in order to fully experience and integrate the entire scope of the Earth experience and physicality. Though it may be necessary to believe in this reality it is folly to think that it is a standalone experience. The universe is vast. Other dimensions may be invisible to our earthly way of seeing so we have to step outside of time and space and allow our minds to open otherwise we remain asleep and oblivious to any other possibility. They say ignorance is bliss right?

Science is turning more to the possibility of finding life elsewhere and actively looking for evidence of it. So maybe in time we will indeed be faced with a reality that for now is only make-believe.

More and more of us are realising that we live in more than one kind of reality and that the multiverse, which is more than one universe, is multilayered with other dimensions.

Lifting the Veil

Waking up to this fact is like peeling an onion, there is always another layer underneath. To lift the veil is to know that we are universal beings, living within different levels of vibrational intensity, intelligence and knowledge.

As each of us wakes up we are then able to help others come to terms with their awakening process which is a natural part of our evolutionary journey. Some are slow to wake whilst others take less time, neither is better or worse, everyone awakens at their own pace. It may take many lifetimes to achieve and will happen once the soul has had enough incarnational experiences of life and prods us out of inertia. It stirs us into opening our inner eyes to what was once forgotten. It will awaken us through unusual and inexplicable experiences in order to get us to pay attention.

Time can slow down our ability to manifest things in the physical dimension and communication between worlds is sometimes like writing a letter in long hand then sending it by snail mail. Whereas without the confines of time it is like composing an email or a text then pressing send and getting instant results. Telepathy is an example of communication outside of time and space and how other beings can talk with us and impart their knowledge, wisdom and love.

When you begin to remember the vastness of consciousness that we are all a part of rather than separate from, then in many ways the physical dimension may seem primitive in its belief structures. The necessary containment of what we consider to be the mind allows us to function daily and is vital in order to gain the fullest opportunities for growth and, to learn the valuable lessons that are on offer to us as humans.

So though linear time can be a hindrance and a

frustration, when deciphering communications from other sources we must take into consideration that time is a human concept and let go of trying to pinpoint when exactly something is to take place. This is particularly important when asking for help and guidance from the universe. Divine timing is not confined to the clock.

The dimensions or realities that make up our world are layered and overlap, and sometimes one reality spills over into another. We may get to experience other ways of seeing, feeling, hearing and interacting with them. These other dimensions include the natural kingdom, where sightings of fairies, devas, little people and other forms of nature creatures come into our consciousness. We usually enter a different state of awareness and when the contact is complete we find ourselves returning to our normal senses often questioning what we just witnessed.

Other dimensions that are often reported as communicating with ours are extra-terrestrial, angelic, and those that include ascended masters and other benevolent Beings that love, help and support our world.

All these alternate forms of awareness are not somewhere *out there* they are a part of our own multidimensional nature. Within each of these realms are layers too. Not all layers are equal, in that some contain beautiful loving energies whilst others do not. In this way life on Earth is a reflection of these other dimensions, some people are loving, kind and compassionate while others are cruel and full of malintent. The nature of personality does not change the minute you die. It may involve a process of learning and purifying before those that have cruel and nasty tendencies see the way forward into a more refined existence.

Let's demystify what being psychic or clairvoyant means. I believe we all have the capacity to sense other realities; it is a natural ability therefore not special in the way that only a few are blessed with it. To believe and promote the idea that some people are special whilst others are not, is divisive and buys into the theory that we are separate from each other and the universe and, it can lead to competitive or envious behaviour.

Being able to voice what Spirit wants others to know is not a special privilege, it is part of the sacred contract that is made while we are still in the spirit realms before incarnating. This contract is made between us and our spiritual advisors who help us discern the best kind of experiences and opportunities to encounter and work with this time around. Those that will add to our soul growth which in turn adds to the overall expansion of the universe are chosen so that we can make the best use of our time on Earth. Not all lives will be what we term good lives. However once incarnate we forget all of that and our guides and spirit advisors may need to remind us in whatever way seems appropriate. They never do anything against our will they simply show us the ways forward and remind us the best way they can that we are not alone. We can choose to ignore their promptings as we have free will. Or we can be so caught up in the illusion of life that we fail to recognise when we are being offered help.

There are amazing demonstrations by people we see as having awesome and special connection to the other dimensions and I applaud them but know this, you have the same capacity as they do. You have extrasensory abilities that you can refine and practice in ways that are uniquely yours if you are willing and are receptive. We all have a thread to sew into the tapestry of the bigger picture and together we make it more complete.

We don't all have the same abilities, each of us is a unique expression of the one consciousness and to honour that fully we must identify and develop our own strengths. Comparisons are deadly and will only bring discontent and pain, so *don't compare yourself with others*. Put your energies into being unique.

We create our own versions of reality all the time. How do those words sit with you? Are you comfortable with the idea that you have the power to create your own reality or do you believe that reality just happens and that you have no control over it? Perhaps you believe that it's all down to the luck of the draw or that you get whatever is predestined for you and you just have to deal with it.

Some of it may be good and some of it bad and that is just how it is but, *supposing that isn't true*. What if the way you perceive your thoughts, the words you speak and what you believe all have a profound influence on what transpires and that by changing the way you interact with your thoughts, words and beliefs you can change your reality—even create a better one. Creating a reality that supports and works for you, rather than against you, is achievable.

Thoughts that you attach feeling to and the words you use have an energy and vibration attached to them that can either enhance or deplete your wellbeing. Energy always follows thought. Though they may be invisible, thoughts contain great power and can be either constructive or destructive depending on how they are focused. Negative thoughts bring negative results; positive thoughts bring positivity and create a better internal and external environment which in turn can create better health and better circumstances. To change your internal world you must change what you believe about thinking and how you view your life and the world. So, have I got you interested yet? I hope so because this is life changing. Once you get the hang of this the world opens up into a more exciting and fun place to be.

The more you know and understand the correlation between thoughts that you engage with, and the energy and subsequent effects of them, the more interesting and exciting things become. If you think the same thoughts repeatedly it becomes like a well-worn pathway of neurons across your brain. Thinking becomes so automated that the thoughts can then lead to habits. This is the case for both positive and negative thought patterns. Automation may be good for machines but you are not a robot you have a soul. Thoughts happen to everyone constantly, we cannot stop them but we can stop attaching unhelpful feelings to them. We don't have to believe that everything we think is a personal indictment of who we are.

If you don't challenge repetitive thoughts they become unconscious and go to a default setting which can be easily triggered at any time invoking similar thoughts and feelings again. As a child you may not have had any control over how life treated you but as an adult you do. You can control how you think, what you choose to believe and how you react or respond to things. Only you have the power to change your internal experiences.

Change can happen instantly or it can be slower, thus taking time before the results become obvious, so be patient and you will see results. The outer circumstances may look the same for a while but your inner world will become richer and more satisfying and, you will have more control about what you allow to influence you. The power is within.

If you feel unworthy, unloved, always fearful, timid or shy it becomes your reality so be careful what you tell yourself because part of you is listening intently. If you allow the opinions of others to sway you to the point of making you miserable ask yourself why you value their opinion more than your own. Why have you given them the power over how you see yourself? Everyone in our life at any given moment speaks to us from their own filtered version of the truth; this doesn't make them right it means that they see life a little differently.

Become self-empowered and then when someone says anything disparaging or attempts to disempower you realise that it is from their baggage and you don't have to carry it. Many people still have emotional wounds from childhood and feel that they are victims of bad parenting and this may indeed be true, but the fact is if you were once a victim, that doesn't mean you have to remain a victim. It is up to each individual to find ways to break away from that mentality into greatness. To find ways to use the lessons learned and become self-empowered and successful in living a *love-filled life* despite the stresses and griefs of the past, is a triumph and is to be congratulated. The only way the past still has power over you is by the constant rehashing of stories that you tell yourself. Become the master that you are and were meant to be, stop whipping yourself with tales of *before* and get into the *now*. Be in this moment, be present, deal with life as it is now.

Don't allow thoughts of *what was* to influence you in the here and now. Be in charge of your life as much as you can but learn to roll with it. No one can control everything that happens, some things are meant to help you learn from the experience of them. Life will throw us many curve balls the skill is in managing them.

The power behind changing beliefs is immeasurable. You can literally change your experience completely and turn things around. This is immense, I cannot stress enough how powerful changing your mind can be.

Being the authentic *you* is both challenging and amazing. The more you are truly authentic the more you will want to be. Enjoy creating a new and better reality and have fun with it. Lighten up, laugh a lot and learn to be a co-creator with the universe. Do what you can to rekindle the joy of living and see the funny side whenever you can. Laughter is a profound medicine.

When I worked as a healer in days gone by I was able to transduce energy into a form that was easily taken in by others. It was used in the way that was most beneficial to them and, that they could comfortably accommodate. My role now is to use these energies in a different capacity. To be able to do this I have had to work on refining and clearing my own energies.

My current role is to pose challenging questions to stimulate you into thinking beyond the conditioning and programming that has thus far dominated your life. Without examining thoughts and beliefs you become stagnant and life continues in an unconscious fashion. I am here to call you out of inertia into wakefulness but it is up to you to respond or not. Either way is okay. I consider this to be a privilege and an honour as well as my service to humanity. Change is constant and when embraced with excitement rather than fear the whole experience is exhilarating.

For our finite minds, trying to understand the universal ways of being is difficult at best, until we reach a point where the egoic mind has to give way and allow a much deeper understanding to evolve. When we look through mortal eyes at the world in which we live much of it makes no sense. Wars, famine, injustices of all kinds and other negativities that surround us can't be seen as anything other than hideous. To even contemplate the suggestion that all is as it should be sounds rather contemptable, and yet from the higher perspective it is.

Even though I can't grasp everything about the universe I have come to believe that it is so and that the universal consciousness is already perfect needing no adjustments from me. We may falter in our understanding and interpretation of it. It does however wish to know itself through us and all other life forms. We have been given free will allowing us to co-create in our own way. So whether we chose to live destructive or constructive lives is up to us.

I know this is a hard concept to wrap the mind around. I have moments where I know it to be true and other times I grapple with the dilemmas of life just as everyone does.

If the universe is pure love seeking to know itself then there is no punishment or damnation. There is only our perception of those things. Heaven and Hell are states of mind that become manifest through both our individual and mass perceptions.

We live by certain moral codes so therefore we judge accordingly, whereas the universe simply experiences everything as we deliver it. There are of course spiritual laws and guidelines, and karma suggests that what we sow we reap.

Eventually we will have to correct the wrongs we did by relearning the lesson. Still there is no judgement attached and we have the opportunity to make amends in another incarnation.

We often reconnect with others from our soul groups who have chosen to incarnate at the same time as us and we help each other in whatever way we can best serve the cause. Sometimes that means playing the role of the protagonist. It is all chosen from the highest intention to be of help to each other.

Having forgotten the original plan we fall into the dream once again. Indignations kick in and we say this cannot be fair or right. The consciousness that created everything is unconditional love and there is no separation between it and us except the separation created by our conditional and limited way of thinking.

Connie Howell

What is reality?
Ask a hundred people and you will get a hundred different answers.
You create your own reality and even then it changes for nothing is constant except change.
Do you choose to remain in your current reality or
Will you be brave and move beyond it into one of conscious co-creation.

Chapter 3

Earth: the great mother

Planet Earth is the mother to all life that resides on it. She is a sentient being who provides for us, her children, with everything we need in order to survive, learn and evolve, and yet we mistreat her and take her bountiful offerings for granted.

Perhaps it is because we lack the understanding that she is a living entity with a heartbeat just like ours and, that we are ignorant of the vital role she plays—we owe her our lives. Worse still is having the knowledge yet mistreating her nonetheless. Without her, life as we know it would not and could not exist. As modern humans we have become fixated on materialism and what we can extract from the earth without facing up to the consequences of the over pillaging of her natural elements. Worse still, we seem to believe such resources are never ending and indefatigable—consumerism is alive and well. We take the attitude that we are at the top of the evolutionary chain and are more important than all other forms of life that Earth's children take.

Cruelty to animals is rife, genetically modifying and chemically spraying our food is common place and polluting our waterways seems to be happening with little regard for the consequences. Concern only for what we can take and profit from leads us into dangerous terrain and yet we still proceed, wanting and demanding more. Rather than understanding the symbiotic relationship we see ourselves as masters and, Earth as our servant. How wrong we are!

When she rebels with natural disasters we pay attention momentarily and call it tragedy but often forget it with the next dramatic news item. We have become desensitised and are not moved long enough to make lasting changes, or we feel that we are impotent against government and big corporations. Of course this does not apply to everyone; many activists are working hard to change the perspectives and outcomes but the majority of us still live as if natural resources were endless and ours for the taking.

I haven't always understood the relationship between us and the earth either; in fact I never gave it a thought until I started to open my consciousness up to things beyond my own selfish needs. Like many I expected that we would always be provided for and that man was superior to all other life forms. I didn't even consider that the earth could contain a life force of its own.

Through shamanic training I learned about the deep connection that many indigenous peoples around the world still have with the earth and nature but which we as westerners have forgotten or deliberately ignore. The natural world has been superseded by what we can manufacture and create synthetically—and we call this progress. Initially I only began to realise this intellectually but the more I raised my awareness the more I *felt* the connection to the life giver we call home.

We receive every conceivable gift from nature yet we always want more, we want to conquer, to be in charge but in the end the great mother shows us she still has the ultimate power. We cannot go on ignoring the responsibility we have to keep our planet clean and alive. Much like our bodies we pollute her with wrong thinking and living. We are out of harmony and out of step with our natural environment; we believe that we are in charge. In the end if we don't change we will pay the ultimate price. We don't own Earth because in reality we don't own anything.

Though we advance in areas of science, medicine and technology we are lacking in a greater effort to look after our home planet. How long can we go on in this way before she wakes us up with bigger and more terrible disasters? Is she warning us to change or perish?

I don't have the mind of a scientist, nor expertise in climate change, I don't know about geology or weather patterns, but I do have access to a wisdom that seeks expression in simple ways that most people can understand and relate to. I am not an activist either, I am simply giving you things to think about and examine for yourself. History shows that changes in climate are a natural process so I don't get caught up in debates about whether or not we as humans are causing the changes that are happening now. I simply look at it from the point of view of being mindful of the home and environment in which we live and paying respect to and for our beautiful planet. It is a privilege to live here not a right.

My husband and I try to be environmentally friendly in that we drive a hybrid car and we recycle as much as we can. However I can still be lured by my own selfish nature towards consumerism and I love to shop, get bargains and travel by air though I admit the lure is much less now. I am still learning to appreciate the earth and my time here, and as I do, my need for materialism is greatly diminished.

We are in a technologically unprecedented time, which

Connie Howell

in many ways is awesome and makes our lives easier but on the other hand our children and grandchildren are becoming more dependent on technology rather than on connection to the natural world and with each other. For the new generations communications are done through mobile phones, iPads and laptops via Wi-Fi. Entertainment is through television and other mobile devices that seem to superglue their eyes to the screens

Food is thought to come from supermarkets rather than from farms and the land that we live on. Governments sell off the land with seemingly little thought for future generations of farmers or local consumers. Food is buried in the ground because the supermarkets don't find it the acceptable shape or size and goods are imported even though many products are grown naturally in our own countries. Meanwhile we become more separated from the actual source of life that surrounds us and that we should be guardians of.

Nature heals us, it helps us breath, gives us joy when we see a beautiful flower in bloom or a colourful butterfly. The melodious song of a bird, the tinkling of a stream, sunsets and sunrises all help us relax and remember, if only for a short time, that *something* other than us created all this.

Nothing is more soothing and renewing than being in nature if only for a day. We have become so disconnected getting caught up in daily routines that often we neglect the part of us that needs solace and communion with the great outdoors. When we are in need of healing for our body or mind, going out into nature is like being caressed with good clean air and a beauty that nourishes the soul.

We can become more grounded just by putting our bare

feet on grass or in the dirt. Paddling in the sea or a stream can give us the sense of being cleansed. Bushwalking or going to nature reserves can lift our spirits and help us remember to breathe in deeply, the crisp, fresh air and be in awe of the splendour of what we see.

All of these things give us the opportunity to let go of the stresses of work and other relationships that we find troublesome or are stuck on. Even if just for a little while the break from the constant bombardment of thoughts can rebalance us and allow us to have insights that a busy schedule cannot make room for.

Birds, flowers and animals, a beautiful sunset or sunrise can reconnect us to the peak moments of wonder about the planet we live on and the source that created it. Even if you believe only in the Big Bang theory there is still the question of why it happened and the awesomeness of the event. Life is a miracle, one that we may never fully understand. In fact I don't think miracles can be understood intellectually. They are felt by the soul.

Nature provides us with constant reminders about the circle of life and death, and though we don't like to dwell on it, we cannot deny it as a fact. We fight it and dread it because we fear death and so we miss out on living a full life most of our waking time. All of the experiences that life throws our way are often shortcut or stunted because we cannot deal with them adequately. Some we agonise about others we may feel fleetingly joyful, albeit in conditioned and restrained ways.

Everything that we are faced with offers us something. The challenge is to find the positive aspects of negative situations. Or better still to feel the feelings and understand

Connie Howell

that all feelings are a valid part of the overall encounter with life. Allowing ourselves to feel our feelings in a genuine way without putting them on the back burner means that we are much less likely to have them resurface later when we least expect it.

A way of turning your concerns over to the earth so that they can be mulched into compost is to write your worries down on a piece of paper then bury it in the soil. If you live in a place where there aren't any fire restrictions you can build a fire and burn the paper. Make it into a ceremony asking Mother Earth to help and assist you in letting go and to transform whatever it is that you have shared with her.

The earth is a living Being.
She breaths and has a heartbeat
Learn to breathe in symphony with her
And new mysteries are open to you

Let your breath be in synch with hers
Be in tune with nature and our brothers and sisters
And you will realise
That we are one family

Like all families some members look a little different
Think a little differently
Or sing songs to a different melody
All are variations of ... Life

Chapter 4

Enjoy everything, be attached to nothing

When Spirit gave me this phrase I understood it completely and immediately. Not just intellectually but my whole body 'got it'. I have always been good at de-cluttering and letting go of material goods but even so I felt the full meaning of 'enjoy everything, be attached to nothing' organically. This includes people and situations. It rang so many bells for me that I actually felt joyous at a level I haven't felt before.

Every day that little sentence goes through my mind and reminds me that we are all here to enjoy life with the myriad of pleasantries it offers but if we become attached to something or someone we lose the freedom of simply enjoying what we have.

Attachment creates suffering whilst non-attachment allows you to enjoy with all the senses and be in the moment—there is great freedom in that. There is no pain nor fear of losing anything with non-attachment, whereas being attached and emotionally invested can be fraught with disappointments and strong feelings. Often attachment is accompanied by the projection of the emotions that we cannot deal with. This keeps us captive and in the struggle. I know that the thought of not having attachment to someone you love will be too much for some of you but that is only because there could be a lack of understanding about what non attachment is. It does not mean that you do not love deeply, in fact it frees you to love unconditionally in each moment. Whereas the fear of loss projects into the future preventing you from fully living and loving now.

Death is inevitable, all of us have to meet it one day and make the transition, so why not enjoy every moment of life now? Try to make every day meaningful in some way. Years of stress and worry, comparisons and competition to see who has the best house, clothes or career is such a waste of valuable time and energy. I have wasted many precious moments myself by being hooked into worry, anxiety and not feeling good enough. It all took a toll on my body and wellbeing. I am now, more than ever, determined to live every day with joyous intent. As you get older and wiser these simple truths become so obvious that you question how you could possibly have missed them in the first place. But that is life, you can't shortcut experience.

To live joyously means to enjoy everything without the attachment of emotional baggage. I readily acknowledge that there are bad things happening in the world, there is nothing new there. Every age has had horrible wars and conflicts. They can be hard to bear especially if they are prevalent in our own lives. The stress can be extreme and all too often it blinds us to the goodness that is also present. Fear feeds fear. If you watch the news or read the papers the ratio of bad news to feel good stories is heavily weighted towards the disastrous and horrendous. Every day we have constant reminders that we live in an unsafe world. Occasionally we see stories that give us hope and faith in the innate goodness of humanity or we escape into movies where even the darkest evil is defeated.

I am not proposing that we live in denial of the dangers

that are evident in the world today but focusing on them increases their potential to impact us in a negative way. If we focus on goodness and do what we can to ensure that we allow joy to be part of our daily business then we can maintain some balance.

By living joyously you can enjoy the food, the clothes, the houses and cars but not be attached to them. This then means you don't feel envious, resentful or jealous of others and you are not destroyed by the loss of any of them. The result being that there is no conflict inside you. If all of us lived this way we could alleviate the suffering, the rampant consumerism and the wanting of more, more, more. Knowing that there is enough for everyone and that we already have enough alleviates the need to grab and run.

All my life I have had a sweet tooth. As a child I never worried about getting fat or sick because I didn't attach any bad associations with the foods. As an adult I fell prey to the opinions of the experts and other people's opinions and so attached thoughts of guilt and fear around loving those things.

Let's face it there are opposing views with every new study and experts can't agree most of the time so what are we supposed to believe? As much as I don't advocate going berserk with sugary treats I do believe that if you enjoy them without guilt or fear then you can occasionally have them without piling on the weight. If you don't have guilt associated with eating then you probably won't want, or need, to have treats as often or in large quantities.

In many ways we are brain washed and don't listen to our bodies, we listen to the opinions of everyone else and end up totally confused. New and contradictory cook books are released with monotonous regularity. Never before have we had so much information about diet, and yet obesity rates are growing daily. The truth is you are the only one that inhabits your body and so you become the expert if you listen to what it tells you. We often eat comfort food to cover up emotional unrest and discomfort so if you work more on enjoying everything and being attached to nothing including hurts, judgements, resentment and pain then the need for comfort eating diminishes. If you slip up with the way you eat forgive yourself and move on.

If you can simply be in the moment you can touch the ecstasy of being one with the universe which is pure joy and love for the abundance of everything. This is how we are meant to live but sadly most have forgotten how to do it. We can never get back the years that have gone so it is important to make the most of the ones we have left. Choose to see things differently and let go of the baggage that often gets dragged around with you. Sometimes we do this with false pride refusing to let go because having lived a difficult life can give us 'street cred' for having suffered so much.

This is a form of attachment and the fear can be that letting go of the known even if it is negative would leave you empty and without sympathy from others. We mistake our baggage identity for our true one. In other words the question is who would you be without the stuff you carry from the past?

Like everything living joyously takes practice. Being in the moment for every single moment is not easy—I can't do it yet. But even if you experience just one time being fully present then you have succeeded in knowing the possibilities of being harmonious with life the way it is meant to be lived.

Connie Howell

It is in the ups and downs, the ebb and flow of life that we find out who we are and what we are capable of. We get the opportunity to develop love, compassion and resilience. We can discover our true nature through adversity by becoming fully aware of our feelings and letting go when we need to. We can maintain the balance by taking the time to reflect, contemplate and work out what truly matters to us. From being fearful we can become courageous, from feeling hate we find that our heart has the capacity to love and forgive.

We will all find the universal consciousness and connect with it in our own way, and in our own time. Values, beliefs and opinions all change as we get older. This is just as it should be with our growing wisdom and experience. As we mature, changes occur in all areas of our lives. We never stop growing so change never stops happening. If we get stuck in resistance the changes are harder to bear and we grit our teeth and hang on with white knuckles fearing that if we let go we will sink into oblivion. Even then if we can embrace the resistance rather than fight it we can find the gold nuggets embedded deeply into life. Knowing that we are resisting and being willing to look at what, why and how we resist life is a huge positive step forward.

No one has all the answers, they are there for each of us to discover within ourselves. If you think you have found the way for everyone to follow think again, that is the ego talking. Each idea contributes to the whole but hang off wanting to convert others to your way of thinking. You may help many by your discoveries and insights but each of us is unique and at different stages on the path of evolution. Ultimately all we can offer others is what has worked for us, the truths we have found and then leave it to their higher selves to inspire and direct them to the next teacher, healer and truth, or better still to the source of their own wisdom. We all have a part to play if we consent to step forward and do our bit.

Life doesn't always work out the way we would like it to. Frequently it is challenging and the opposite of what we want. We may feel disappointed and let down by the universe or by our internal guidance system. I have had my share of disappointing results but if life is about fully experiencing everything then disappointment and even failure is part of a necessary learning curve.

Feeling is a key component of how we experience things but hanging on to feelings can be a source of suffering that keeps us trapped in the past. Self-righteousness, anger, resentment and indignation are powerful anchors to situations that are often best let go of. Once we loosen the grip on things gone by, we can maintain the rhythm and momentum of forward motion toward the goal of evolution into a more enlightened state of awareness. Sometimes we get so caught up in the emotion that we can't see the lesson behind it and end up going around in circles—I am an expert at circling.

Expectation is the real cause of disappointment. Life simply brings us various scenarios to see what we do with them. At the end of the day it is the human part of us that feels the feelings, and often they can result in emotional fracture. The Divine part of us was, is and always will be intact.

Being present, focusing on the now rather than projecting back to the past or forward to the future, keeps us from suffering the angst of what was or what might be. This way we can experience the joy of each moment as a new experience, unsullied by the detritus that has accumulated over time. The pollution of past hurt and pain makes us want to project probable outcomes onto the future based on what we previously experienced in the past. The thoughts and feelings that were generated by our reactions to those events still influence us in the here and now. This means we miss the present opportunities because we are too busy projecting either backwards or forwards. Therefore our energy is already coloured with whatever emotion lays dormant and unresolved.

Things that should be obvious are missed because our attention is elsewhere and our energy is scattered leaving us unmotivated, scared and stuck in the revolving door of automatic responses.

All things come and go, we cannot hang onto them forever yet so often we become obsessed with ownership and entitlement. Holding on serves no one, least of all the self, yet it is a common problem shared by most of us. The angst of letting go because we fear loss means we tend to avoid dealing with the fear.

Lack of understanding that even though fear has its uses, it can also immobilise us and cause much heartache by preventing us from achieving our goals, means that we may miss the opportunity to grow through facing our fears and moving beyond them. If we then add feelings of inadequacy to the mix we have a merry-go-round of underachieving or giving up entirely. It can be both a blessing and a curse, for fear can motivate us to try harder and do better or it can stop us dead in the water, too afraid to move on and risk encountering more things to dread.

Having experienced much to be afraid of in my past I know all too well the deleterious effects on the body and mind. I am not afraid of fear anymore though I still experience it. I can look it in the eye and ask why am I feeling the way I feel? I realise that fear is not my enemy. Fear of the fear is the true enemy and one that I held onto for many years. As I became brave enough to feel the fear without turning away and with the knowledge that I would survive even though it felt all consuming, dissipated the constant worry. I became self-empowered and no longer driven by out of control emotions.

I honour fear as part of life and know that it can prevent us from leaping off tall buildings or putting ourselves in harm's way; it is a safeguard when we listen to its signals to avoid real physical danger. Fearful thoughts have taught me much and I am grateful for having felt them to the point of panic because when I learnt to master them my self-confidence grew exponentially. I learnt the valuable lesson that to feel the feelings as they occur and to deal with them in the moment means they don't get subjugated and come back to bite you in the arse later. It hasn't stopped me from feeling fear but now the fear does not stop me in my tracks.

Whatever feelings come up for you deal with them now, don't put them off until later because later can be a long time coming and the feelings will have expanded. Feeling what you feel now wholeheartedly allows the energy of it to be free to move without pooling in some unseen corner of your mind or body. Though some feelings are hard to bear, just allowing them to be there without resistance is liberating in the long term because you don't carry unresolved issues with you as you move forward. You realise that you can survive even though it may feel painful or scary and you become the master rather than the slave to your emotions.

Anger is a volatile and powerful emotion that makes us want to act, maybe even lash out at those we feel anger towards. When you engage with anger or other reactive emotions you move out of centre, become unbalanced and you can easily get involved in power plays. Anger may make you feel powerful and in control but in reality you have lost both control and power, and as a result you can strike out at others either physically or verbally. Conversely if you are unable to express yourself the anger gets swallowed and lives somewhere in your body. Sometimes anger may be justified and is a true reflection of how you respond to certain situations but all too often anger is a cover up for how you really feel. It may make you feel powerful when in essence you harbour feelings of being dis-empowered. Being attached to the righteousness of how you feel will only hold you back.

If you were to remain centred, you would stay fully connected in your power and nothing that someone says or does would affect you. You may agree or disagree with what is being demonstrated but by maintaining non-attachment nothing will knock you out of centre and into reacting rather than responding. For the record, I am a long way off mastering this myself.

Often beneath anger is another kind of emotion that is hard to face such as grief, sadness or pain of any kind. Anger can mask those feelings. If each of us were able to deal directly with such things as they arose, anger would not erupt and cause negative reactions. If all of us could remain centred and feel empowered it would eliminate the need for greed, rape, robbery, intolerance, road rage and all other negative behaviours. Sadly, not many of us were taught how to deal with, or appropriately express strong feelings, as they arise. We simply got programmed by a long line of ancestral reactions to life.

A frequently asked question is: 'Why does God allow destructive things to happen?' The simple answer is that it is our own free will that determines how we act, think and feel. We are responsible for the destruction so instead of blaming God we need to take responsibility for our own actions. We come into human form not to be at the mercy and whims of any deity or dogma but to learn how to love and co-create, as well as, to remember that we are all part of divinity. Let's stop blaming the parent and take a good hard look at ourselves.

Attachments to life and all that it brings can crystallise feelings into dense energy forms which can later develop into illness, energy blocks and the inability to manifest what you want. Through dismantling these kinds of energy blocks good health can return. Right thoughts, actions and good living will restore balance and harmony.

Try to make every day meaningful in some way, even if it is in the tiniest detail. There is nothing worse than getting to the end of the day and having the feeling that it has been wasted. You can't ever get that time back so make the most of every moment whether you are simply sitting and reading, having a nice cup of tea or watching the world go by. Enjoy it all. If you are a super busy person, always on the go, stop for a few moments and reconnect with the pure joy of being in union with the life source that surges through us all.

Practice gratitude daily. Gratitude is a form of prayer. It tells the universe that you appreciate all that is offered to you.

It is a mark of respect and connects you deeply to Divinity. I have written about gratitude in my previous books, it comes up all the time for me as an important reminder that life really can be good.

I don't always receive everything I want but I am always given what I need. Even before I understood about the power of gratitude I had some good things happen to me. As I work with it consciously now I am more able to attract what I actually want, and what I want now is quite different to what I would once have requested.

I don't yearn for material things now. I respect the fact that I have everything I need and am comfortable. Some of the happiest and most humble people I have ever met are extremely poor compared to our western standards. For me inner happiness and letting go of any attachments are the greatest gifts of all.

When you genuinely feel gratitude the heart centre expands and you can embrace life in a positive way. Fear and worry make all the energy centres contract so feeling grateful is a good way to feel the expansion and wholeness of who you really are.

Gratitude is a willingness to experience the love that the universe has for us, to acknowledge and pay homage to the immensity of its power. How is gratitude different to love? I believe that gratitude is an aspect of love and the more you practice it the more open you become to love by directly engaging with the universe.

Try to find at least one thing today that you are grateful for and if you can feel it deeply you will engage in a sacred connection with all that is, and remember that feeling attachment to anything is fear-based. Choose love.

Lifting the Veil

Nothing is permanent
Everything dies, that is the circle of life
But if you live every day
When the end comes there are no regrets
You will have done and had everything you needed
To be all that you came here to be

Material things can be taken, lost and destroyed
Enjoy everything without grasping
The greatest treasures are unconditional love and compassion
With these no attachment is possible
And no loss ever

Chapter 5

Resistance: friend or foe?

Feeling some sort of resistance is often a signal that we have somehow tapped into an area within ourselves that needs deeper healing. Being resistant is almost like pulling the curtains closed so that no one can see in and you don't have to see out. I don't think resistance is necessarily a bad thing, short term, as long as it is not left unexamined because it is signalling that something needs our attention.

The soul has many ways in which it communicates with us. The difficulty is in knowing *how* it specifically communicates with us. Sometimes it takes a bit of detective work to find how it uniquely speaks to us in ways that we can understand. Do you know how resistance speaks to you? What kind of language or signs does it give you to get your attention? How does it alert you to the fact that something needs to be looked at in greater depth? Is something gnawing at you but you can't quite work out what it is?

Sometimes feeling resistance is a clue that something or someone is not right for you. Other times it may purely be a defence mechanism telling you that the situation is too confronting right now. Only you will know the difference as you examine what is really going on inside you. Are you aware enough to even know when you feel a genuine resistance to something or someone? Are you being stalked by a feeling or an idea that just won't go away?

Lifting the Veil

When I feel resistance I feel it in my gut, my body tenses up and it is usually because I feel threatened in some way. Not a physical threat but a psychological one that is telling me that I would have to stretch myself beyond my current version of reality. Or alternatively I might sense that the situation is not right for me and I must listen to that. At other times a feeling may be accompanied by anger because my nice little 'safe' world has been shaken, or because my ego gets in the way and gives me a trillion reasons why I should not change my views. Usually this indicates an unwillingness to let go of preconceived ideas to allow an opening of my perception. As much as I love discovering new insights there is a part of me that likes to hang onto the known rather than venture too far out into unknown territory. My comfort zone often doesn't like being nudged and tested, and sometimes I dig my heels in and have a hissy fit.

The energy of resistance shifts when the true feelings have been discovered, acknowledged and worked on. Resistance is one of many opportunities for growth if we allow it to reveal its hidden depths and treasures. We often don't like change as it can be threatening to our sense of self and the world we have built around ourselves.

Healing the self from a lifetime accumulation of pain and negative experiences takes a multilayered effort to both recognise and release. Added to that is the fact that there is so much anger and unfettered hatred in the world today that it makes it all the more difficult to allow our vulnerabilities to show. To step outside of the madness and stay sane in an insane world takes courage, and diligent effort to stay present and not get dragged into the many dramas that unfold daily. Not getting hooked into other people's issues and opinions helps.

People will defend their beliefs and prejudices with vigour, as if only their opinions are right and have merit. Unrestrained ego and power tussles are rampant and are taken over with verbal clashes that often and increasingly result in violent or volatile reactions.

What has happened to mutual respect? It seems to have been overridden by the constant fight to be right and the illusion that there is only one way to survive, thrive and live. Tolerance is missing in a lot of our daily interactions. In our recent times the most aggressive wins gets the upper hand and acts of violence on unsuspecting and innocent bystanders increases with every news flash. Often the psychological prize is in being seen to be superior. These ideas come from an inner feeling of lack in one's life and come from our more basic and primitive survival nature. Surely we have progressed beyond the 'I'll get you before you get me' attitude, and yet day after day we see the results of violence and the need to dominate not only in greater society but also in our homes.

It serves no one to suffer in silence or to retaliate. What is necessary is to step out of the madness and into the calm of one's soul, the higher part of us that knows only love.

As humans we have become addicted to suffering or to inflicting suffering on others, and like any addiction we have to take it one day at a time to break it down. Some days shine like flawless diamonds and some days are just downright rough. Being calm when everywhere around us is in turmoil takes enormous effort and dedication to move beyond it all. Being able to recognise our propensity to get caught in the ever growing circle of drama takes awareness. Understanding

Lifting the Veil

that part of us sometimes invests in staying in the circle is even harder and flies in the face of common sense. Yet we do because it gives us some kind of pay off. It may be that we get sympathy and attention from being a victim and we don't know how else to get what we need.

The more awake to our true nature we become the more we are able to step back and witness events, rather than participate and become caught up in the struggle for power and dominance. We can be in the world but not of the world. I wish I could tell you that I don't struggle with life anymore but the fact is I do.

All my spiritual knowledge and insights do not preclude me from the human experience. I have moments of elation and know that I am exactly where I should be and other times my humanity overwhelms me and I think about ageing, death and the possibility of being alone. Then I can succumb to doubt and fear.

All of these are illusions that the ego continually throws up until we become mature in our attitude towards all things human. Coming to terms with the violent ugly side of human nature is difficult and can be overwhelming and distressing.

I know that in essence I am an immortal spirit with a universal consciousness and yet I can still feel the strong pull of the human conditions that we all share. I can be swallowed up by the dichotomy, the duality, and the in-betweeness of being neither here nor there and yet knowing at the same time that all is exactly as it should be. This is one of the challenges of being human, to transform and lift our consciousness in surrender to that of our universal self and our higher consciousness where real change takes place in our lives. But how do we do it? In my early days of spiritual learning and searching I would devour books that described ways to inner peace and how to contact the spiritual realms.

Phrases such as *let go, go with the flow, the answers are inside you* and *God dwells within*, were signposts of how to progress towards a better understanding, but they were mere words and phrases to me until I learnt to integrate them and put them into practice. Now when I feel that I am resisting a situation I try harder to see the root cause of the feelings and deal with them at that level. Change is scary.

I used to have trouble working out how to relax and breathe into my resistance while a psychological war was waging inside me. Where was the magic wand to suddenly convert my thoughts and feeling to those of peace, love and serenity?

Let me save you some effort here, it happens when it happens and usually isn't a single bolt from the blue that makes it all clear. Nor is it your constant *go to default setting*. It is more likely to be a series of 'aha' moments sometimes months or years apart.

You cannot hurry spiritual growth beyond where you are ready to be. The illusion of time is complex because we see it as linear and it is hard to get past the idea that we live within the confines of time. We need to change the way we view our thoughts. Instead of trying to change them, which usually involves struggle, it is beneficial to simply watch them and not latch onto them. So in essence they have no meaning they are just thoughts. It isn't until you attach some feeling or meaning to them that they become troublesome.

Spiritual advancement needs a continuous dedication and a willingness to keep on keeping on even when it feels like you are going backwards. It is not for the faint-hearted and it has to become a way of life not a sometime or a one-time thing.

Workshops, courses and retreats are all immensely rewarding and can be enormously helpful but they are pointers, you still have to do the work at home. There is a natural high that we get listening to leaders and teachers as they show us the possibilities available, but don't expect to have the same experiences that they may have had. If you do it could lead to disappointment because we all experience things in our own unique ways.

Even though the *X-Files* series told us 'the truth is out there' it is in your inner world where it actually exists and as you progress in your enquiries you may even ask yourself if there really is an 'out there' at all. Or is it part of the collective dream that we call reality? Ponder that for a while, it is sure to boggle your mind.

Make your own discoveries, find your own truths—don't just accept what I or anyone else says. If it doesn't feel right then it isn't right for you and it may never feel right for you. There are numerous paths all of which lead to the same destination so enjoy walking your own route. You might even clear the path for others to follow, but they must tread it freely and in their own time. The gift of teaching is to show the possible ways forward and then leave it to the individual to do what they will with what you are offering. In fact the only thing we can ever teach another is *how to remember.*

Doubt is a subtle form of resistance that we all encounter sometime throughout our life. But don't be fooled, though it may appear subtle it gnaws away with great diligence. Sometimes it is a constant companion other times it seems to float by occasionally. Try not to hook into it.

When working on our spiritual growth doubt often appears because our sense of what is real is challenged.

Old conditioning can be stubborn and ingrained so shaking it off is difficult. We may put some of our experiences down to imagination which is thought to be part of a fantasy world or wishful thinking. Imagination is a tool that gives us great imagery on which to focus our desires. Manifesting what we desire first has to have a thought then an image. You have to know what it is you actually want rather than have a broad idea that is too wide and scattered.

So, far from being *just imagination* it is a creation waiting to be made manifest through focus and intention. The problem for most of us is that we cannot hold the focus long enough and so we dismiss the idea altogether. Then resistance kicks in again because we may feel that manifesting our dreams doesn't work for us.

If you feel that you are not a visual person and therefore cannot get a clear picture, imagine a lemon or an ice cream. I bet you can do that without any difficulty which means that you can do imagery but you may not be able to concentrate and narrow down exactly what it is you desire. If you take it a little further with the lemon or ice cream you probably will even feel your mouth water a little so you have not only visualised it but you have imagined what it tastes like. This is successful focus and if you can do it in this instance you can repeat the process with other things. So give it a go, start with small things and work your way up to the bigger picture.

If resistance comes in any of its forms like disbelief, frustration or irritation just watch it, feel into it and see what exactly it is that you are feeling then work from there on releasing it. Sometimes, though we ardently desire something, there can be a background program at work such as long held feelings of not being deserving or that it is greedy and wrong to have abundance when others do not.

Resistance will have many faces and disguises and it is up to you to work out what yours look and feel like. Nothing is more certain than the fact that change is our constant companion, so if you can learn to embrace it rather than fear it, life will be smoother and the challenges more doable. Sometimes the good old days just have to go to make way for today otherwise we miss a whole chunk of life.

Connie Howell

*Resistance has its place but don't let it become your permanent home
Continuing to resist the changes that can bring growth and benefit
Simply makes the job harder than it needs to be.
Learn to bend with the wind*

*As you bend you become more pliable to the challenges of life
And change is less threatening and more pleasurable
You realise that you will not break
So you let go and enjoy the wind, allowing it to take you higher each time.*

Chapter 6

The Collective Nightmare

What is the collective nightmare and how do we know if we are in it? If you feel any kind of doubt or uncertainty about being part of a greater consciousness and you feel, fear, anger, hate or other negative emotions that make you feel separate from the universe: then you are in the collective nightmare. Don't feel bad, we all are until we wake up and snap out of the dream. Before we incarnate we have all agreed to be immerged in the illusion so that we can learn the lessons of being human. Then when we are ready to become aware of the fact that we are spiritual beings having a human experience, the illusion starts to thin out and we emerge from the trance-like state into awareness.

Once you realise that you are asleep you can start to work your way out by choosing to see past the illusions that are so deeply entrenched in our thought processes. Our belief systems and hand-me-down opinions from family and cultures can then be challenged and we can emerge from them.

My personal experiences of being trapped in the nightmare are many but the ones that stand out come from fear. I grew up with anxiety and the propensity to worry. I bit my nails relentlessly throughout my school years. When I left school at the age of fifteen I somehow managed to drop the habit. However even now if I snag a nail and I don't have a nail file handy I can go into full bite mode.

I had times of normal bravado and confidence during my teenage years but underlying and ever present were the silent entities of fear, accompanied by feelings of inadequacy which erupted into panic attacks during my late twenties.

I found the anxiety and panic attacks to be torturous and more numerous with time. I could not escape them as they were internal. As a young adult I smoked, and then when I gave that up I took up eating as a form of numbing the feelings. When the feelings of anxiety and panic peaked I feared I would never be able to free myself of them, and the prospect of living that way for the rest of my life saddened me and in turn was a source of more worry and anxiety.

It was like an ominous cloud hanging over me. I believed I had no control over my thoughts or my life. This is when I began to explore books on spirituality and health. I wanted to educate myself about my condition so as to have the feeling of more understanding, as well as to be proactive in getting better rather than being medicated. I gained insights into alternative ways of looking at life and I learned about things such as being one with the universe and having the power to make changes from the inside. My locus of power became internal rather than external. This is a simplistic explanation of my long and ongoing journey towards enlightened living and freedom from the prison of my negative programming.

I want to explore the feelings of anxiety with you and tell you how it was for me. Although anxiety is seen as a form of mental illness, I prefer not to view it that way as it causes stigma and self-consciousness for those that suffer from it. For me anxiety is a state that results from trauma of some kind and from the thoughts and feelings that have been internalised about the traumatic situations.

Often the true source of the concern is unknown and so anxiety latches onto all kinds of things and makes them the focus. Thoughts become more fearful and constantly drone on whether at the forefront of consciousness or in the background. Always alert and watching for impending panic attacks the mind and body get little rest. The 'on' switch gets glued down and it is hard to relax for any length of time. Sleep is affected while the mind and body are always alert. It is fatiguing trying to hold oneself together but you still have to function as best you can.

When anxiety becomes chronic it is much more than the occasional bout of butterflies or simple worry and it can reach into every aspect of your life. It happens for a reason but the reason may not be the one that seems obvious—it goes much deeper. It is often the result of painful experiences as children that we are simply ill equipped to understand or deal with and so the stress becomes anxiety. It may show up in youth or lay dormant until something triggers it later in life.

The symptoms of anxiety and panic vary but are plentiful and include unpleasant sensations such as palpations, sweating, feeling light-headed and like you might be having a heart attack. Shortness of breath and being unable to concentrate on anything other than the symptoms are also clues that you may be having a panic attack. You might have to rush to the toilet often accompanied by feeling nauseous. Of course many of the symptoms are similar to physical ailments so knowing the difference between anxiety and illness is difficult at first.

If you suffer from anxiety and panic disorder you

actually start to fear the fear. The symptoms feel so awful you become afraid of having them again. The more you are afraid the more frequently they arrive and affect more areas of your life. In some instances they become so disabling that they prevent you from leaving the safety of the house. The fears become a phobia.

At some stage in life you may have experienced events that were too hard to handle because you were either too young to deal with them or because you simply didn't know how to resolve them.

Unresolved feelings don't just disappear because you aren't consciously thinking about them; they remain in your body and can trigger responses that seem exaggerated. They can catch us by surprise. The have an energetic input that, left unchecked, can affect our health and when they surface they are often magnified. For instance we may find ourselves erupting in rage at the smallest things rather than being appropriately angry or perhaps we feel more afraid of something than we would normally be.

When feelings make themselves known it is necessary to deal with them there and then rather than letting them sink back into oblivion because sure as anything they will get triggered again and again.

Sometimes it can take years before we become aware of something that occurred way back which we set aside at the time. It takes effort and energy to look at the work that has to be done and to be constructive with what comes up.

An issue doesn't always simply disappear right away either, it may take several rounds of working on it. Our unresolved issues are often multilayered and sometimes need to be dealt with one layer at a time. Each time we clear a layer we move closer to restoring balance.

The body will often alert us to some issue that is held in the subconscious by creating an illness or disorder. Sometimes this may be major while other times it is a simple but frustrating matter. If you can tune into what the body is really trying to tell you, even though it may seem cryptic, you can get to the bottom of things more easily and release what needs to go. When you suffer from any kind of illness it is hard not to identify exclusively with the body, this is part of the nightmare. We become hypnotised into believing that the body is who we are. The body is the house we live in but it is not our true self. We need to keep our house in good order and learn through the experiences it presents us with.

The world is filled with fear in all its various forms, fear of terrorism, poverty, illness, death and you know the rest, you will have a long list of your own. Together if we buy into that fear we keep the collective nightmare going and can feel utterly powerless. The journey out of this is individualistic. Those that have gone before us have shown that it can be done. We are not alone on our quest to find better ways of dealing with life, though we may often feel isolated. Many of us are now in the process of awakening but it will take a greater number to tip the scales in favour of peace and cooperation.

Fear and hate are prevalent in all walks of life and it seems that the smallest things can make the fire combust into explosive behaviours. You may ask the question *what can I do?* If we only ever ask that question without following up with some sort of action nothing changes. We remain either impotent or in denial. There are those who readily promote fear and hate and both are catching. Before we know it we can become wrapped up in the sticky web finding it difficult to get free whilst waiting to be eaten. But we must be free of the hysteria if we want to be agents of change

It is tough going, I know. I try to avoid the news rather than getting entrenched in the enormity of negative occurrences that are beamed out to us via the media. There is a fine line between being informed and being overwhelmed.

No matter what seems to be happening on the surface try to focus on the goodness of humanity. I personally would rather be on the team of the illumined than batting for the other side. Try not to lose heart and don't leave it up to others to fix; we are all in this together. Overcome your own demons and touch that place within you where only love resides. This is a worthy and effective offering that really makes a difference. The more of us that focus on love the greater the impact and contribution we make to the world.

There are many examples of what we consider good and privileged lives, when we think of royalty and celebrities we tend to categorise them in this way. We only see what we want to see and believe. We cannot know the depths of their inner lives or the personal thoughts and feelings that they have. We can all too easily put up great walls between us in the form of 'us and them' judgements. Envy and jealousy erodes us. They cause increased feelings of separation and keep us in the mire of collective mis-thinking.

The Universe means for us all to live good and productive lives not just the chosen few, but until we can agree on the undeniable fact that love, not hate brings peace to the world we will remain in chaos. We have had many leaders in the field of enlightenment and spirituality over thousands of years but yet we still struggle with finding inner peace.

What we can do once we are free of the illusion is turn to others and offer our hand to those still oblivious to the fact that they have all the power they need inside themselves and that it simply needs to be recognised and accepted. I hate to say it but most of us are addicted to suffering.

Because we suffer and don't yet have the key to transform it into a more positive experience we may try to rob others of their power by criticising, killing, ignoring and judging.

We do this out of ignorance of the fact that we are already powerful enough without having to wrestle for more. If we simply take a deeper look inside and challenge the demons of our past, the hurts and pains can be more easily forgiven.

As we realise that those who hurt us were also acting from fear, not love, then we can become open to compassion. This in itself can be an enormous challenge but if we want to be free we must at least try. Whatever haunts us must be faced with courage and then the power it had over our lives is nullified.

We have been indoctrinated into the nightmare by those that didn't or don't know the truth of who we are. If you believe life is hard and there is no way out then that will be your reality. Energy follows thought and what you put out is magnified coming back to you in an ever increasing spin cycle of nonsense.

I can only tell you this because I have been in that position many times. Even though I am in the process of waking up I can be so easily enticed back into taking a nap.

Connie Howell

Sometimes the nap is longer than others and I have to remind myself to wake up again and stay awake.

Waking up and realising that you are divine is usually a gradual process as you slowly become more cognisant of the dream. You can easily become seduced back to the collective by watching the news, listening to gossip or being involved in the spread of fear. Don't give up just keep on prodding yourself to stay awake and ask the universe for help. It will bring you many interesting ways to wake up. I know that it is hard to stay focused on the good things and on choosing love over fear but the more you do it the quicker it will become your first response. Be as authentic as you can by matching your thoughts with your feelings and actions, and the world will be a better place. Am I there yet? No not fully but I am well on my way, are you going to join me?

I try to be the witness of my life rather than being so engrossed in it that I forget all that I have learnt. I know at the deepest level that I am a soul having an incarnational experience not once but many times. However sometimes life drags me back to the semi-unconscious state and I can get lost in the drama of daily details time after time. It doesn't really matter. The fact is I am conscious most of the time. I am constantly learning new ways to tap into the field of awareness and to bear witness to how the ego loves to create drama over the smallest things and, if there is nothing going on, it will invent something.

I used to believe that I had to quash the ego and its rantings but now I understand that it is not my enemy, it has its place and purpose. From this position I can befriend it with a higher understanding and awareness and work with it rather than against it. I don't tolerate its foibles but I also don't castigate it. I try to look at what is really going on and when it seems to be pestering me I can respond in a more mature way to whatever comes up.

I haven't mastered it yet, I can still have fits of childish outbursts but I am much more aware and can ask myself the right questions in order to move me in the direction of real growth.

Connie Howell

Wake up it's time to see the universe
It is reflected in every one you meet
Look into their eyes and you will know
If they have cast off the slumber of illusion
Or if they need to sleep a while longer

If they respond to a gentle nudge
You have done your job
If they sleep on leave them and let them be
Their soul will arouse them when the time is right

Chapter 7

Love as a vibration

Everything has a vibration and one of the highest and finest vibrations is unconditional love. When we think of love in an everyday way, the love that we feel for our partners is what often comes to mind. There is also the love we feel for our families, friends and pets. However unintentional, we can contaminate this love with expectations of one kind or another and therefore our love becomes conditional.

Universal, pure, unconditional love is a concept in our minds that we may aspire to but we *aren't quite there yet*. I know that I am definitely not even close to attaining it the majority of the time but I have glimpsed it. With unconditional love there are no expectations, no conclusions, no demands there is simply an outpouring of pure unadulterated vibrational energy. This energy can cure anything, fix anything and heal the world—if only we could all demonstrate it, embody it and become one with it—which is what the universe wants for us. Being already in perfection, the universe through you and I seeks the diversity and growth that imperfect experiences as human beings can bring to it. So in that respect there are no mistakes, no matter how much your rational mind wants to dispute it.

We know that enlightened beings and teachers from history, and current times, speak about unconditional love and how it is the ultimate goal for us all. We are surrounded by it, come from it and it is the true essence of what we imagine the creator to be.

Why is it so hard for us to accept it and let it into our psyches then? Ego and programming have become obstacles preventing us from attaining it. Chastisements, criticisms and contaminated beliefs handed down the familial and ancestral lines are all in the way. It is for each of us to clear away the detritus of life little by little until we can see the possibility of entering into that stream of glorious consciousness that true unconditional love is.

Sometimes we cling to relationships long after they are productive and stay in destructive ones because we don't know how to move forward. Fear can hold us back from making the decision to move on. We are convinced that we will never love the same again but on reflection find that love is a moving growing energy that can come many times in different ways. All we have to do is allow it and be receptive to all possibilities. As we release old patterns of behaviour we can let ourselves be more receptive to the delights of what love offers.

As much as we want to bring people forward with us into new growth sometimes we simply have to let them go. Staying in any relationship whether it is a marriage, work related or a family dynamic can become toxic and unhealthy.

What about the relationship to ourselves? Let's take a look at a common crutch that we use when we feel bad. Emotional overeating is a frequent way of numbing how we feel. Suppose eating could take on a whole different meaning. Instead of denying yourself nice foods or loading the eating of them with guilt you simply enjoyed eating with no hidden agenda and no self-recriminations. How about instead of

Lifting the Veil

eating sweet foods to sweeten up your life because it is the only way you know to find comfort, you simply ate with gusto enjoying every mouthful, savouring the flavours and delicacies for the mere pleasure of it. Instead of being a crutch to lean on, food can become a joyous event that nourishes your body rather than putting it under strain. It will be a source of good nutrition rather than a way to numb your silent longings.

Eating without the emotional blackmail and self-recriminations will give health, pleasure and a feeling of gratitude to have such an abundant variety of beautiful foods without having the aftermath of disgust. Eating would simply be eating without negative emotional input, no guilt or shame, no gained weight.

Food is just food but the thoughts and meanings that you place on it are crucial so attach love and let the food transform itself into light and energy in your body. Let it imbue you with vitality and satisfaction. Look at all the other methods you use to numb emotional pain and you will be surprised at the variety of distractions you can come up with in order to placate the feelings you are trying to avoid.

What am I saying here? If you allow yourself to feel your emotions and not run and hide from them then there will be no need for binge eating. You will have faced the good, the bad, and the hidden, and have no need to turn to food or any other addictive substance to feel better or elevate your moods. Food is not a substitute for friends or companionship.

Feel what you feel in the moment, face it, deal with it and there will be no residue carried over to your next hand to mouth experience. If you have difficulty doing it perhaps you can find someone to help you.

As always I write from personal experience I will give a potent example of how unresolved feelings affected my daily life.

I experienced recurrent urinary tract infections for a while. From a physical perspective it is not uncommon in a woman of my age but I felt frustrated and somewhat distressed at having to use antibiotics each time an infection occurred. They knock the system out of balance and it takes a while to become stable again so though they can be necessary I felt conflicted about taking them. I have trouble with taking some alternative medicines as I am sensitive to many of them.

I know without a doubt that the body reflects emotional issues. This knowing has come through experience both as a natural therapies practitioner and as a spiritual enquirer. So I knew that this area of the body can reflect being pissed off about something or someone. I have a good loving relationship with my husband so I knew it wasn't him that I was feeling off about. As I allowed myself to look into my feelings about myself and my femininity some interesting stuff came up.

I make no secret of the fact that I was molested as a young child but I have dealt with that and moved on, however the general pattern of being sexually exploited followed me for many years in various ways.

I remembered being at the movies with my mother when I was aged seven or eight and a man came to sit next to me. As the movie started and the lights dimmed in the theatre I felt his hand moving up under my dress. I pulled away shocked and he hastily retreated. By the time I was turning to

Lifting the Veil

tell my mother about it the man had disappeared into the dark.

Many years later, as a young adult, my future father in law one day started sliding his hand up my leg supposedly in fun and when I protested he said, 'You like it'. This projected 'blame' made me feel shame which I then internalised. I did this with most of my unsavoury experiences with men because I felt powerless and as the fault was always supposedly mine I believed it.

I didn't take it any further, it was his word against mine and I knew he would find a way to dismiss it. I had never learnt to stand up for myself and speak out. So in a way I was an easy target, I was young and inexperienced at dealing with these things in a firm and positive manner. Instead I pushed the incident out of sight and out of mind. Though the conscious mind might forget an incident the subconscious holds on to all of our memories. These can surface when you least expect them.

My step father also had designs on me and boldly asked me to have sex with him. I was in my twenties at the time and his requests appalled me on all counts. Thankfully I was able to tell him not bloody likely but I never revealed to my mother his demeaning and lascivious behaviour.

How could I tell her and risk ruining her life? My mother had suffered greatly most of her life. Her stepfather had made overtures to her and then after she married my father she was beaten regularly after he had been drinking. In her early forties she had cancer and went through radium treatment and was extremely ill, I feared that she would die.

I was around the age of eight or ten, I don't remember exactly but children were not included in the chain of information. I think I got to see her once briefly while she was in hospital and I never forgot the impact of seeing her so ill, so vulnerable and in such pain. With all this in my emotional kit bag I was even more disgusted with my stepfather as he had seen her go through this ordeal. A part of me came to detest men and their sexual cravings.

Even though I was capable of having relationships, the pain of my past caused deep shame and guilt about being a sexually attractive female. If I did enjoy sex I was made to feel like a fallen woman. There were many more times that I was propositioned or taken advantage of and I was often the topic of gossip and innuendo. Some of it was founded in half-truths and some was totally fabricated. There were times when my behaviour actually deserved the bad press as I acted out the part I was cast in. You become what you think you are. If you think it long enough you believe that it is true. So I had many sexual encounters over the years.

The guilty and shameful feelings about my sexuality lay beneath the surface for a long time but were always ready to pounce. Though feelings may be pushed down and forgotten they do not go away and they unconsciously affect current perceptions. Even though it seems like the past is tucked away it often comes back to bite you on the bum, or in my case, the urinary tract.

As I grew spiritually I began to look at healing the deep shame and guilt feelings that had accumulated and I did heal much of it. I forgave others where I could and moved on. However I never really healed and forgave myself for being female, powerless and sexual.

So back to the present and the UTIs, I had received a lovely massage from my friend Amanda. I had decided to do what I could to regain health and balance and try to circumvent the infection cycle. The day after the massage I had the memory of the man at the pictures and my father in law. Then others memories surfaced. They weren't new memories but I hadn't thought about it for a long time and was only thinking about it now because of the recurrent issues and my desire to clear the pattern.

When I tuned into how I felt I realised that I had no respect for myself or my feminine anatomy. I was angry at those parts of my body because, once again, they were causing me trouble on a regular basis. I also touched on the anger I felt at being exposed to the violence that my father perpetrated on my mother, and by osmosis, onto me and my siblings.

For a time we lived with my father's mother and sister so there were six females plus my father and brother all living in one small house. My grandfather who died before I was born was also a violent man and so we were all disempowered from an early age.

Not only did I feel little respect for my femininity, I also resented the fact that part of it was literally sick and being a nuisance. I felt angry that I had not had any *powerful* female role models in my family to teach me self-respect. I knew that I had subconsciously blamed my body for all the unwanted advances and experiences that had dogged me throughout life.

When I really thought about it I began to see that it wasn't my body that caused these things to happen it was the perpetrators lack of respect and general disregard for women. My body simply responded to my perceptions and fears about being me.

Connie Howell

Finally (I shouldn't be surprised by it as I am writing about the vibration of love) I was able to look at loving the feminine side of me, thank it for its creativity, for birthing my children and for giving me pleasure. For allowing me to be soft but powerful in a non-aggressive way and for being part of the sacred feminine energy from which I can forgive my past. I can even silently thank the perpetrators for facilitating the lessons that I needed to learn in order to fully embrace my feminine energy. I can see that although the females in my family were victims they also had strength and courage to face each and every day and I love them for showing me strength in the face of cruelty and humiliation.

I was then able to thank the recurring infections because as a result of having them I was sent for an ultrasound on my bladder and kidneys and a small kidney stone was found in both kidneys and a benign lesion was on the right one. None of which required any treatment, but once again the universe gave me an early intervention rather than letting me go on to have worse problems and I had the opportunity to heal myself at a deep level.

When I realised this I felt such love for and from the universe, and unequivocally knew that I am not alone, that the universe has my back. I have been able to go deeper into my subconscious and dig out other issues, and set about loving my body rather than seeing it as the *enemy*.

I need to rely on food less to stuff down those feeling of shame and guilt and I am becoming whole in this aspect of my life. Because the body has a denser vibration it takes a little while to catch up in vibrational frequency with inner development but at least now my mind and body are on the same page. Once again I have been shown that I have a team of loving spirit friends and advisors at my side as well as those on this side of the veil.

I caught a glimpse of the eternal self that is unconditional love. I am not yet totally connected with it but I am working on it with a newfound energy. We are all capable of connecting with such love but few of us have reached that state yet.

Fear often envelops love and only when we can release the fear rather than get drawn into its web do we feel the depth of love that resides inside. Of course fear often has a part to play and the natural inclination when faced with some health or other crisis is to be afraid. At the core of our being we are love, pure love. If fear covers over the doorway to the heart we find it hard to access this love and in fact may not even realise that the pure vibration of love is there. We can learn to access it if we go deep into silence or contemplation.

There are so many things in life that we believe we should be afraid of. The ego teaches us well to live afraid rather than rejoice in the experiences that life offers us every day. Challenges become something to overcome rather than an opportunity to delve into and connect with the essence of who we really are. Finding ways to meet the challenge with balance and calm are ever present if we allow ourselves the luxury of self-discovery. We are more powerful and resourceful than we know.

In coming to know myself as a spiritual being living in a physical body I have noticed how much fear lives inside me and how, on examination, I find that it is simply a group of misguided thoughts that constitutes this fear. Breaking it down from an overwhelming mass of accumulated thoughts is liberating and empowering.

Once we recognise this we have the power and impetus to release the fear and move towards finding the Divine self. Nothing has ever felt so beautiful to me as that brief moment of connection and knowing it is possible allows me to go forward with the knowledge that fear doesn't have to be conquered it merely needs to be faced and released. Let it go and transcend it. This may have to be repeated as the ego will not surrender the tight grip of impending doom and catastrophe so easily.

It doesn't matter what faith you follow as long as you don't become steeped in dogma and you remain in the aspect of allowance. Allow others to have a different path than you: there are many. We each need to find our own way on the road that is best suited to our soul's specific evolution and purpose. Love is at the core of everything but we forget this so easily, getting caught up in believing that our way is the only way. Agree to disagree and let other people have their own belief systems which may even strengthen you in yours.

The universal source created all things, so we are not separate even though on the surface it looks that way. Faith, religion, spirituality are all tools to find what is right for us. What you do with them makes them loving or turns them into persecution.

There are many ways in which we witch hunt each other because of our beliefs. Lack of tolerance and understanding are major weapons in castigating one another. Fear as a foundation on which a set of beliefs are based is a powerful motivator in trying to 'save' those who do not follow the path we think they should. Though this may seem well intentioned it can be incredibly destructive in that it casts those with opposing views as either in need of salvation or as the enemy.

I have had experiences of my own spirituality being questioned, instigated by fear and religious fervour. In the past I have been accused of having evil working through me because of my views. At the time I was devastated that such accusations and superstitious nonsense were directed at me. I was a volunteer giving a loving service but the fear that others had, overrode all the goodness I had demonstrated. I am not alone in my experiences. Still to this day anything not understood or outside the confines and narrow parameters seen to be the 'way' are cast out and denigrated.

Connie Howell

Vibrations are all around us and in us
We are constantly vibrating
Let's vibrate our whole being with love and acceptance
And sing the song of the beloved

There are many paths to follow
Choose the one that is right for you
Follow your heart and listen the Divine Self
What else could you possibly need to find the way?

Chapter 8

Learn to read the signs

So often we are given signs from the universe yet we fail to recognise them. The universe speaks to us every day in many ways, some of which are so subtle that we miss them. It might be that we are unconscious to what the finer energies are telling us or because the signs are so simplistic in nature we dismiss them as unimportant. We have spirit guides, angels and a whole network of spiritual beings that we can call on for help. If we could see behind the veil we would be amazed at the vast array of aid that is available. It is all too easy to feel alone and miss or misinterpret the clues that are sent our way.

If we ignore the signs given to us then we may get the unmistakable kind of *in your face* correspondence. Chances are that if you are waiting for a voice from the heavens to speak to you then you will most likely be disappointed but if that is the only way to get a message through to you then a voice may indeed be used to get your attention. This however is not the usual way of messaging accessible to us on a frequent basis.

It takes effort from the other side to break through the dense layers of physical reality in order to communicate with us, so we need to pay attention. This being said, it doesn't mean you should try to see messages in every minor detail. That would not only drive you nuts but also everyone around you. Sometimes things are simply what they are without any hidden meaning.

No one can really teach you how to read signs from the other worlds; it comes with experience, awareness and being open. We each receive things in our own way. Some may see or hear whilst others feel things. We also have varying ideas about what constitutes a sign. What is a message to me would seem obscure to you. A feather found by me may be a sign that spirit is wanting me to pay attention and tune in but to you it is just a feather dropped by a bird.

What is obvious to me could seem inconsequential to you. We all have a unique sense of what the messages we receive mean. They may share similarities in form and can be archetypal in nature.

I have an eclectic mix of traditions to call on. Having studied many kinds of wisdom teachings signs come to me through sources such as nature, clairaudience, telepathy, clairvoyance, books, and films, conversations with friends and through my dreams. There is no limit to the amount of ways that spirit can connect with us. I listen to my gut instinct or intuition and I know that even though I may not understand at the time, the meaning will be revealed eventually. Not knowing but still trusting is an important communication builder and is strengthened with practice.

Not every event in every day means something, some days are simply monotonous and mundane, and that is okay. You can work on lifting your awareness to synchronicities and other consciousness raising methods that you feel drawn to and that work for you. By doing this you make yourself readily accessible and more able to pay attention.

Always one to be practical I look for things that can enhance my connection to spirit and the universal consciousness. We live in a physical reality and it is often through this dimension that objects and people are utilised to interact as intermediaries. I am often prompted by other people, who may be oblivious to the fact that they are giving me a message, that I may not otherwise have recognised or received.

I have also seen people who are totally oblivious to the signs that they are being given but which seem so obvious to me. If I know the person I may give them a hint but it is ultimately up to the individual whether they choose to notice or not. I can sow seeds but often don't see them grow. I believe though that sometime in the future if the person is willing the seed has the potential to become something beautiful and things will unfold exactly as they should.

I have to admit that a lot of signs that are given are not easy to understand. This can be frustrating and I often wonder why the meaning can't be immediately recognisable, but that is the way it is. Spirit language isn't the same as our everyday earthly language and it has to traverse different vibrations to connect with us.

Signs can come from nature in the form of feathers, animals, flowers and nature creatures. Also through dreams, conversations with others, visions, telepathy, gut instincts and many other unique and fascinating ways. An interesting sign that I was given came to me after contemplating one night as I lay in bed. I was wondering how to stop the incessant chatter that crowds the mind and go into that deep calm place where we can enter into communion with the universe. I pondered on it as I was going to sleep.

A couple of days later as I opened the curtains in the lounge room I saw a large insect on the outside of the window. I couldn't work out what it was in that moment. It was too big to be a cricket and not skinny enough to be a stick insect. I asked my husband if he knew what it was and he told me it was a praying mantis. As soon as he said that I recognised that it was indeed a praying mantis.

We had lived in the Blue Mountains for eighteen years and I had never seen one in or around the house so I knew this was a message for me. I had never seen a praying mantis at all before, except on television programs.

I looked up the archetypal meaning in my animal totem book and was overawed by the fact that the praying mantis represents stillness. In fact they stay absolutely still for hours on end. So my previous thoughts and questions about finding the calm place within were being answered by an example from nature. This type of synchronicity has been a factor in my life more times than I can remember but each new time still fills me with the joy of being in communication with the universe and the diverse ways in which it communicates.

The praying mantis stayed for two days on our window making sure that I had really received the message. I never once saw it move, what an incredible example of stillness.

Other signs are more difficult to decipher and I have to admit sometimes I get utterly frustrated at knowing there is a message there but that the meaning remains elusive. Because the universe doesn't speak in the way that we do, it makes understanding what is being transmitted akin to looking for a piece of a jigsaw puzzle: you know it is there but can't find it yet. When you do you have to make sure it fits in the right spot. Often it can look like the piece we have in our hands is the one we want, but when we place it with the other pieces it isn't quite right. All I can say is relax, don't try too hard and the meaning will eventually become evident. The fact that you recognise that a sign is being given to you is a splendid first step. If you still don't get it, the universe will find another way to reach you.

Lighten up, it is easy to get bogged down in *getting it* right away but the universe is patient and will find another way to show you what it is trying to say. Have fun, treat it like a treasure hunt, be grateful that you are given the opportunity to tune in, and be aware that you are part of a two-way conversation.

One of the more amusing ways that I am contacted is by our doorbell being rung by invisible hands. At times though it can be a little disconcerting, like when it rings at three in the morning. Thankfully it is rare when this happens.

I have had to learn the difference between ego chatter and the prodding from spirit which I often get in the form of a nagging thought that just won't go away. I have to decipher the nuances of either being nudged or being drawn into an egoic drama.

Sometimes the signs and symbology that come from a spiritual source are so subtle that it takes investigative skills that any detective would be proud of. Not one to enjoy the mind games that the ego indulges in I try to view it from various angles so that I know I am being guided by intuitive thought streams.

I have been on the spiritual path for most of my adult life and have learnt and grown exponentially but I still feel bamboozled at times, so don't despair if you too are experiencing these things, for whatever spiritual path you choose to follow it will be an ongoing journey of self-discovery.

Connie Howell

With time your understanding will deepen, your trust will grow and going with the flow will be so much easier. Your sense of reality will change, challenges will still come but you will feel more able to handle them. Ask for help from your inner resources and listen from your heart.

Listen to Nature
It has much to tell you
Beauty to show you and
Harmony and balance between life and death

Listen carefully
Attune your ears to the different language of Spirit and
Learn a few key words to understand at the deeper level
From your heart not your head

Chapter 9

Getting Real

Being genuine and being authentic is what I refer to when I use the term *getting real*. This is not as straightforward as you might think. We have many ways of disguising the differences between what we think and what we say. To be real you have to *mean what you say and say what you mean* and you have to acknowledge the difference between thinking one thing and saying another that seems more acceptable. Often we try to couch our true thoughts by placating the truth so as to not hurt someone's feelings or so that we can be better thought of.

We may want to be liked and accepted so we moderate our behaviour accordingly. This creates incongruent feelings within us and the start of inner turmoil. The more we engage in moderating ourselves the greater the likelihood of inner conflict at having adopted a false identity. This conflict is inevitable because regardless of how we behave we ultimately have the desire to be accepted as we truly are.

Being genuine takes a considerable amount of honesty and courage. On the whole we want to be readily accepted and liked but we don't want to hurt or offend. So instead we may pretend to mean what we say when in fact what we feel could be quite different. The truth is you cannot really lie to yourself. Your body is intelligent and stores the truth of how you feel. If there is resentment or irritation behind having to fake, deny or hold things in, your body will know it and feel it. In a sense it is a kind of self-betrayal and a disservice to the other person.

So though you may think you are doing the right thing by not being offensive or saving face, because you are unable to tell the truth you may in fact be laying the groundwork for disharmony inside. Things buried can have a nasty habit of resurfacing later at the most inappropriate time. Holding on to anger, resentment, irritation and other strong feelings can fester inside. Mind and body are interconnected so they will affect each other.

Find ways to break through the layers of denial and projection that lie deep within you. At least be honest with yourself, no one else need know your secrets. Your spiritual growth is between you and your soul.

Allow yourself the luxury of self-examination without going to extremes and you will find a way inward to where the treasure of whom you really are, without all the conditioning and baggage, is buried. When you get past the inner criticisms and the hand-me-down beliefs, it is like seeing a lotus emerging from the mud and being bedazzled by its beauty.

We all carry burdens and expectations from the past. Perhaps we wish we had done things differently and behaved in a more positive way. We seem to lose touch with the innocence and purity that we are born with and easily accrue feelings of regret, shame and guilt if we have stepped outside the box of 'acceptable behaviour'.

If we failed to have our boundaries respected and intact as children we may blame ourselves. The self-recriminations can be harsh and brutal but sometimes we need to know it simply wasn't our fault. The expectations that we have about the way in which we *should* have behaved when in fact we couldn't have been different are hard to shed but shed them we must in order to be a healthy adult. The ongoing thoughts of *what if* and *if only* are distressing and disruptive to ongoing maturity. Let them go they serve no purpose and only keep you stuck.

Getting real and being congruent means feeling and acting brave even when you may be feeling afraid and would prefer to do nothing. This does not give you license to be offensive to anyone whenever you feel like venting and it is not to be misused by dumping your feelings on unsuspecting people.

Being authentic means being responsible for your own feelings, knowing that they are triggered but not caused by anyone else. The feelings are already present in you somewhere, others may unwittingly push a button that has been glowing red just waiting to be pressed and ignited. In some cases the button purposely is pushed by those who want to cause a greater impact knowing that these are your vulnerable spots.

Being accepted and liked are two very powerful motivations and to avoid having our buttons pressed we may tell white lies or flatter someone to gain their acceptance. Our need to fit in is a powerful force that can cause us to step outside of our authenticity. To be genuinely accepted means accepting ourselves and knowing when we are playing the game to get emotional strokes to inflate our ego. It feels good in the short term but unfortunately it is never enough and so the game goes on.

Sometimes we may fake the truth because we are afraid

of losing something or someone precious to us that we love. We may feel that we have to be nice to a boss when really we feel the opposite way but are afraid of losing the job. Or when we have the fear of losing a partner we may circle or evade our true feelings altogether.

All of us feel fear and anxiety at some point in our lives but for some it is a constant companion that regularly interferes with clear thinking and clear decision making. If fear can be identified at the root cause rather than at the superficial level, then real progress can be made to heal the issues behind the fearful thoughts.

Feelings, especially strong ones if not dealt with appropriately at the time, will keep on determining the way life pans out. What we focus on grows. Our actions can become fear-driven rather than thought out in a rational way. It isn't easy dealing with what have sometimes been life-long behaviours.

So the question is: do you believe you are worth the effort to take the steps that will enhance you and alter the trajectory of your life by changing how you think? If the answer to this question is 'no', then your life will probably continue on in the same way. Left unchallenged your thoughts will keep on in the same old cycle and accumulate more of the same.

Positive life changes don't happen by magic they need awareness and acknowledgement from us to get the party started. One of the things you can do, to begin with, is to investigate where certain beliefs and ideas come from. You could ask yourself the question, *whose idea is this? Was it passed down or do I really believe it.?* Or another great question is, *what age am I when I think this?* This will help to determine if it is the adult version or a younger part of you that is responsible for the thoughts.

Sometimes when I do this I can identify that it is the child within me who is in charge. I then have to bring back the control to the adult part of myself while acknowledging that the inner child is frightened or angry. If it is the child showing up and throwing a hissy fit then doing inner child work can really help. Many years ago I learned a hypnosis technique called Alchemical Hypnosis which helps you to find and rescue the inner child and nurture it so that it knows you have its back and that it is being heard and is safe.

Alchemical Hypnotherapy has four major components. These allow us to access powerful internal resources within the subconscious mind to affect real and lasting change. We become more empowered to tap into latent healing powers within us by:

Rescuing the child
Contacting our guides
Past life regression
Conference room therapy

Rescuing the child helps us to explore forgotten memories from childhood to find the source of wounding experiences that impacts us subconsciously through feelings such as repressed rage or abandonment issues. By bringing the child into the present we can meet its needs properly and by nurturing and loving it in a constructive way the child can give up creating tantrums or other drastic ways to gain attention.

Contacting our guides gives us the opportunity to access our richest resources and work with them in a way that helps us connect with valuable information that normally we may not hear amidst the background of constant chatter in our heads. Guides are sometimes called Archetypes and are energies that we can tap into and utilise for healing ourselves. Our Higher self is by far the wisest guide but all our guides can have a beneficial input and can be utilised in accessing greater wisdom and understanding.

Past life regression can often help us to pinpoint traumatic past life experiences that impact our current lives. We can process difficult emotions associated with the past life by returning to the time and place to gain the understanding and insight that helps us to release the hold it has on this present incarnation. We may also tap into *past life contracts* and even change them or release ourselves from them.

Conference room therapy gives us the arena to work with sub-personalities. These are the many voices we have in our head. Some of them are the inner child, the lover, parent, judge, and critic. I am sure you can identify many more.

In the conference room we can become conscious of the different voices we carry and can choose between them to create a forum where meaningful discussion can take place. We can also invite wiser, more influential voices such as guides to the table.

For more information on Alchemical Hypnotherapy you could go to the website www.alchemicalinstitute.com there you will find information and a list of teachers and practitioners.

When I practised Alchemical Hypnotherapy back in the 1990s I was privileged to see people connect often for the first time with their inner child. It was profound for both the client and for me to witness this meeting.

There are many methods of doing inner child work and really it is about finding one that suits you the best. You may want to go to a therapist or try it for yourself. I believe that it is wise to have at least a few sessions with a trained therapist in whatever method you are attracted to as they can guide you and hold the space for you to discover both the wounded and the wise parts of yourself.

Letting the inner child control how we think and act is not a good idea except when purposely letting loose and having fun.

I recently came across a fabulous book called *Grow Up Your Ego: Ten Scientifically Validated Stages to Emotional and Spiritual Maturity* by Jeannette M Gagan, PhD. This is an amazing book that explains the different stages of development that we go through and what happens if they are not met correctly.

There are exercises with each chapter that, with practice, help us to bring the ego to the maturity it was always meant to have. I found this book incredibly helpful, you might too if it calls to you.

At times it feels impossible to find our way and to stay on our chosen path. There are so many interpretations of what the purpose of life is. It is important to develop a strong connection with the *still, small voice within*. Some call this intuition or a knowing.

You will recognise it by its ability to guide you to higher awareness and to the right information at the right time. The more you tap into this source of wisdom and understand its unique method of interacting with you, the better chance you have of responding to life rather than being at the mercy of reacting to it.

Lifting the Veil

Who am I today?
Am I living from my real self or my adapted self?
Do I speak my truth or hold my tongue?
Do I lie to myself and others or do I have the courage to be real?

Am I a child or an adult in this moment?
Who needs my attention right now?
Can I love myself in all the stages of myself?
If not I then who can?

Chapter 10

The big picture

As humans we have a tendency to view life from the limited perspective of the ego. We are convinced that only what we can see with our physical eyes, hear with our ears and feel with our fingers, is reality. The ego will do anything to keep you small and to stay in control if it is not properly matured. When threatened it will serve up the best logic that makes you question the validity of all things that can't be verified by the intellect.

This point of view cuts us off from interacting with other realities. Some things defy logic. Of course to live in this world we have to believe in what we see because we have purposely chosen to incarnate specifically so that we can experience this dimension and all that it holds.

The ego is not the enemy and doesn't need to be defeated but it does need to loosen its grip so that we can fully experience alternative realities without thinking we are going mad or hallucinating. One of the roles the ego plays is that of protector so that we remain safe from harm.

At some time though, we have to be willing to let go of the limitations that are set by the ego and transcend them. Refusing to open up to other possibilities keeps us locked in the overall illusion that the material world is all there is.

In the scheme of things it probably doesn't matter, after all there are many more lifetimes to be had aren't there? But why suffer the separation any longer than we have to? You may have a good life and feel that it isn't so bad to be here, but perhaps there is even more to be had. I don't mean more material things, although there is nothing wrong with that so long as you don't allow them to define you.

There will always be people that want proof either scientific or otherwise and who will insist that there are other explanations for the kinds of experiences that I and others have had. I cannot offer any such proof nor do I particularly feel the need to do so. For me direct experience is enough, I trust but not blindly, I am a practical person who has had far too many instances of other interactions for them to be hallucinations, wishful thinking or the machinations of an over active imagination.

I can assure you I do not have any underlying mental anomalies that I know of. Doubters will still doubt and the believers will go on believing. The naysayers will have logical reasons to explain the unexplainable and give plausible alternative explanations. That is the nature of things.

What I do find disturbing though is the vitriol with which some people state their case against those with opposing views. As much as I don't always agree with the beliefs of others I know that we are all called in different directions and that is perfectly fine. Free will is a beautiful thing.

The Soul will call us forward into possibilities and new ways of experiencing and thinking while the ego resists and wants us to remain in the safe world of the familiar. So what are we to do?

What I do is remain grounded and practical. I don't feel the need to choose between this reality and the spiritual ones.

I can interact with both. To do so requires a firm connection to my earthly home and my physical body. From this grounded position reaching into other dimensions is achievable and coming back to this reality is easier.

Have you ever had a dream where the characters and the setting of the dream feels so real that it takes a while to work out if it was just a dream? What if it is possible that we ourselves are characters in a dream being dreamed and imagined by the universe?

We may feel real and are indeed convinced that we are who we think we are. But what if we and this world we live in are in the consciousness that created everything? In fact you could say we may be figments of the universal imagination.

Now this may take some convincing even if we are willing to allow ourselves to ponder this possibility. It is a stretch I know, but worth thinking about. Sometimes we must allow ourselves to ask unanswerable questions.

I believe that all writers of spiritual material can offer no real, concrete proof of what we write about. All I can do is share with you my experiences and understandings with the utmost sincerity. It is then up to you to see whether what I have said resonates with you or not. If not then you should discard it.

No one author has the insight and answers for everyone, and the diversity of thought and beliefs is one of the many blessings in life. Rather like diet books with information on healthy living the information can be confusing and seemingly contradictory. One person gives one theory and another seems to have an opposing view. Ultimately we have to judge for ourselves and see what

Lifting the Veil

resonates individually for we are all unique. We have different body chemistry and emotional needs. We are also at varying stages of soul growth.

One of the attributes of free will is that we each have the freedom to choose what to believe. Though it is often difficult to sift through all the different ideas, if you do it from the heart and with intuition you really can't go wrong and you will find the right path—for you.

Acceptance and willingness to allow each individual to go their own way is paramount if we are to practice unconditional love and surely that is the ultimate goal. For in unconditional love we find our true selves and allow others to be themselves without wanting or needing to change them.

Sometimes a spiritual teacher comes along and you choose to follow them. Teachers are not just the guru or leader in the field of metaphysics. You and I are teachers, we are also pupils. A person you look up to and that you feel has the knowledge and experience to move you forward in your understanding can either serve as a guide or even an irritation.

Remember how the oyster makes the pearl? Not everyone that serves us is someone we like or that lives up to our expectations of what a teacher ought to be. They may trigger strong emotions and even disappoint us. They can make us question ourselves and our beliefs. This is a good thing. For anyone that you perceive to be more powerful than you is really a reflection of how you lack the connection to your own power.

To put others on a pedestal will often result in a fall from grace, eventually shattering the spell of enchantment that you have cast on yourself.

True teachers and leaders don't seek admiration they

serve us by being authentic and facing us with our own projected feelings. This is for the highest good and serves humanity in the purest way.

Of course some of our teachers are people in our lives that we dislike. They are often family members or partners that challenge us in ways that we would rather not experience.

Lessons aren't always easy or pleasant but they are always for our higher learning. Whatever emotions are evoked, be they negative or positive, are emotions that already lie within you. No one can make us feel anything but they can push our emotional buttons.

There is movement going on. The universe is stirring, growing, expanding and it wants us to go with it, after all we are all a part of it, one with it. If we are having a hard time it isn't because we are being punished and if we are having a great run it isn't because we are being favoured. One experience is a reflection of what needs to be healed the other is indicative of what has been healed.

It is hard to fathom the universe with our minds, sometimes you just have to let go and stop paddling so furiously and simply allow the flow to take you where it will. This may seem counterintuitive to someone who needs to feel in control but it is the unknown that truly bothers and frightens us. We are on a big adventure and we are all invited to participate. It is meant to be an exciting and exhilarating ride. It is only our resistance that makes it seem bumpy. If we let go and trust in the universe it won't let us down and we may even find ourselves squealing with delight.

We are all part of the tapestry of creation
Each of us has an important thread
When all the threads are woven together
There emerges a picture that otherwise would be incomplete

Together we form a beautiful scene
With all our differences and colours of various hues
A community beyond that of our small town or village
We are a community of Souls

Chapter 11

Building Trust

Children trust implicitly until they are betrayed and their trust is shattered. The road back to the place of unreserved faith in humanity can take a lifetime or more. As we mature we must learn that trust becomes a choice. It can be a hard one to make, and may have to be done one step at a time, especially when faced with tough situations. The inclination is to be too scared to be vulnerable again. I unequivocally understand this. I have been in that place many times and I have been faced with the choice to trust or to stay with the memory of the pain from the past rather than move forward.

The fact is when trust has been broken we too in part become broken and we lose touch with the knowledge that we have choices. Often the damage done can leave us with the idea that we are powerless or that our choices are not met with respect. So we remain vulnerable to the will of others when we are in similar situations.

We may have to relearn how to make the choice to speak up for ourselves in a way that makes it clear that we have boundaries that are not to be crossed. We can use the honouring of ourselves as a means of rebuilding self-esteem. Then we will be strong enough to reinforce our boundaries whenever necessary. If your self-esteem is diminished it can be restored.

Sometimes choosing to extend yourself to believe in

others and more importantly your self seems unachievable—but the fact is you can. Each time you choose trust over fear you become stronger and more empowered. You may lapse and have to start over. That is why this chapter is called building trust. It doesn't happen all at once, especially if the hurt and pain that you carry is significant. Each time you find the courage to trust you build up strength for the next time.

Abuse of trust, such as the type that happens with the exploitation and mistreatment of children, causes immense damage. Finding the will to trust again is like trying to climb a mountain without prior training. It seems impossible but the human spirit, coupled with the soul's strength can get you through.

There are so many variations of trust issues. An important one is learning to trust yourself, especially if you have made mistakes or if you believe you have been the cause of your problems. Victims of abuse often blame themselves rather than the abusers.

One of the biggest hurdles I had in life was how to rely on myself when I hadn't been able to protect myself or others from harm. As a child there was no way I had the maturity to avoid exploitation nor did I have the necessary understanding of why things happen. As a result I made some bad choices later in life. No amount of inner searching made it any easier to forgive myself for being foolish. I was of the opinion that there was something intrinsically wrong and unforgivable about me.

So how do we choose to move forward in future circumstances when we already hold false ideas about ourselves? Whether we have been the betrayer or the betrayed it is equally hard to live with. Most of us have experienced both sides of the equation at some point in our lives. So not only do we need to know that we can trust others, we also need to know we can trust ourselves to act right, do right and heal the past.

Making mistakes is an integral and important part of life that helps us grow and mature, however living with the fall out can be embarrassing, shameful and load us with guilt. Having others exploit us by purposely abusing our trust then lying about it can cause deep anger and rage. Resentment, fear and other powerful emotions become deeply embedded in our psyche. These are hard to deal with. Some may never recover and become impotent and crushed not knowing how to move beyond the trauma.

I find this sad, but I understand it. However trust is a choice that gives us courage to try again and to re-establish our shattered self-esteem and sense of power. I made the choice to heal because living with the pain was no longer viable for me. I do not mean to imply any judgement on those who find themselves stuck in the past. I believe that there are all kinds of help available, but we need to be ready and able to allow it into our shattered lives.

We never really know another person's life path or their pain and suffering. We can't know the reasons behind their choices; we don't walk in their shoes. To trust means being willing to take risks and be vulnerable.

When dealing with unseen dimensions trust comes one step at a time. It is hard when we seem unable to consciously interact with these invisible dimensions and it will test our version of reality. All our lives we have been taught to rely on physical perceptions, so to step outside of this stronghold will take some time as well as a willingness to be open to other possibilities.

When you are used to dealing with the world intellectually and rely on the physical senses, surrendering the intellect can be frightening. It can also be exciting and liberating. Allowing the ego to step aside, opening to the universal communication and the way in which it reveals itself to you is in itself amazing. To then have *unbelievable* things become believable through direct interaction is like nothing else.

Like many of you I have had trust issues that were hard to break free from. That is where choice comes in. You can either decide to stay immobilised by your lack of trust or you do what you can to pick up the pieces and go forward.

Worthy of your attention is your own intuition and insight when dealing with others. Then, if you come across people who seem untrustworthy, you see it for what it is rather than automatically coming from a place of mistrust This means it is nothing to do with you being vulnerable because of unresolved trust issues but more about their lack of capacity to be truthful and act decently. Not taking things on board that belong to someone else is also a valuable factor in gaining self-trust again.

I am acutely aware that there are many people out to grab what they can and to scam us, mistreat us and generally take advantage. If you stay strong and trust your intuition along with your strengths and values then you are well on the way to seeing through scammers immediately.

You don't necessarily need to be overly sceptical or constantly on guard. If you have built the inner dialogue with your 'bullshit detector' then you can rely on the signals it gives you. No doubt there are times when we may fall short on that

Connie Howell

front because there are masters of deception everywhere but pick yourself up and know that you can still trust yourself and that sometimes we need to have reminders about the lessons we are learning.

A key lesson is not to take anything too personally but rather try to see the bigger picture. If you can do that then things are less painful, less dramatic and occur less often. Depersonalising takes you out of the victim role and into the observer role.

Lifting the Veil

If you choose to trust
When once trust was broken
You show great courage and belief in the overall goodness of life
No longer a victim, you become part of the greater good
You become a leader, a way forward for those yet to make the choice

Courage is not constant
But what is constant is the need to choose to be courageous
When really you would rather run and hide
As you keep making the choice to be brave
You show me that it is possible

Chapter 12

Rewrite your story

In our collective illusion we believe that we are stuck with the story of our life. So we harbour the thought that we just have to suck it up and make the best of it. The fact is you do have the power to rewrite it—starting now. In essence we are creators and in that capacity we can do just about anything we set our minds to. No matter what has happened in the past you can change the trajectory of the future by changing the way you perceive life. You can change from victim to active participator.

By using vision and persistence you can put an end to tales of woe and the reasons why you can't do things. The ego loves to narrate all kinds of dramatic scenarios in our heads. The time comes when you simply have to stop buying into feelings of being powerless and start taking charge. No one can do this for you, it's up to you. When you take the first steps you will find that the Universe will be synchronistic in bringing you who and what you need to help you develop the skill of co-creation.

Change is inevitable so why not visualise the change you want rather than dreading what might happen. Thinking that a situation will never change is a drawback because it involves the feeling that you have no control. You will remain stuck in the circumstances that are being experienced now. Beginning this moment is where to start the process of

Lifting the Veil

imagining new and better conditions. Each moment is a new now and therefore a fresh opportunity to establish more fruitful patterns of thought. If external conditions really are beyond fixable right now you can still imagine a better outcome. The outer world often reflects the inner one so change from the inside will in some way be reflected in your daily reality.

Words are powerful even if they are in your head and never leave your mouth. There is an energetic frequency behind them. You may not vocalise the thoughts but that does not mean that the energy behind them somehow magically disappears. If you latch onto any thought it becomes magnified, that goes for both positive and negative thoughts. Energy is real, whether or not you see or feel it. Don't be seduced into thinking that thoughts are meaningless, especially those programmed by constant repetition.

I don't think any of us can monitor our thoughts all the time, but the ones that make the most impact are those that we add emotion to. These are the ones you need to be mindful of especially when negative or critical about yourself or others. An energetic path develops and becomes an automatic response. It is a misconception to think that we can stop the stream of thoughts. The fact is every one of us has a constant stream of chatter pumping through our minds. Not hooking into them is the challenge.

To change the circumstances of your life you first need to be aware of what it is that you want to change and why. To rewrite your story you need to be clear about what your existing story is. What programs are playing in the back of your mind stuck on the repeat cycle? Once you have investigated that and are clear about it you can see what needs to be changed.

Start by imagining the life you want. Allow yourself the luxury of daydreaming. If you want more money, for example, envisage the lifestyle you desire and imagine how it feels. Imagination is a vital factor in manifesting what you desire.

A word of caution, if you desire something that is not for your highest good or something that may harm others it will come back to bite you so keep it clean. Maintain the intention that it is for the benefit of all.

So back to the subject of money, which is what most of us worry about, and which often may contain different and inherited ideas passed down to us. Imagine how life would be easier if you could pay your bills, travel and have the freedom to help others if you so desire. Visualise creating a solid financial foundation for your life. Only feelings of doubt about being deserving or that it is impossible to imagine your dreams coming true will prevent you from doing this successfully.

My thoughts around the laws of attraction have changed as I have grown. We often begin with the emphasis on attracting material things. It can be fun and of course it can be life changing. I find nothing wrong with this but it can keep us stuck in wanting more stuff. If we were to focus on being peaceful and in harmony with our greater good then most other things will be taken care of naturally.

Wanting to acquire more materially can be a symptom of deeper needs that haven't been identified. It is worthwhile to examine where the longing comes from. I have nothing against material goods but as I get older the allure is no longer on what I have but rather on what I am.

No matter what the outer world shows us there really is enough wealth in the universe for all of us. You being wealthy doesn't mean that you have to take from someone else in order to add to your cache of prosperity. If you feel strongly about those worse off than you, then when you create your new story, you can be as philanthropic as you like and help them out in whatever way seems appropriate. When you are financially secure you can offer help from an unconditional space.

Of course money isn't everything yet most of us want to be more secure in our finances. We believe that this leaves us mentally and emotionally free to create better lives overall. Do you have to believe your story when you rewrite it? Well it would help, but after a lifetime of living one way then suddenly changing direction can be a hard concept to digest. Practice makes perfect so keep on visualising life as you want it regardless of what the outside is showing you and you will see signs that things are shifting. Once the shift begins a momentum carries it forward into manifestation. Remember you are a creator so why not create marvellous things rather than mediocre ones?

Do I think it is simple? No, not at first because our ego and our resistance really kicks in making doubts form in the mind. It is easy to be discouraged and fall right back into the pattern of the life you are trying to change. When this happens get back on the proverbial horse and start again. There are many helpful things that you can do to support your efforts. Make a journal dedicated to the things you want with headings such as 'wealth', 'health' and 'better relationships'. Use clips of inspirational sayings that you find helpful and stick beautifully inspiring pictures onto the pages. Note down the names of authors and books that inspire you. Write down any experiences that support your endeavours, log synchronicities and thoughts of gratitude. These are all tools that can help you.

You need to be consistent and persistent with your new stories. Old habits die hard and our patterns of thought and behaviours are often stuck on default so it takes consistency to make permanent changes. But you are worth the effort aren't you?

If you don't invest faith and trust in you how can the universe move you forward? Work with it and recognise the changes whether big or small. Some results will be swift and others will take longer. You will need to keep at it until you are living the life you choose.

Monitor your dreams for clues. Some dreams seem nonsensical while others can be clear cut in their messaging. One of the things I do is to imagine who I am without all the defences and barriers that I have accumulated throughout life. Who is the real me? I ask myself how my life will look if I allow myself to *be me*.

I can see that all the shields I erected were the result of hurt and pain that I had been unable to process. Being too young, feelings of shame and guilt or simply not knowing how to deal with what happened all got in the way. As always, new insights came in time and in response to my inner requests to be free of the past.

I went inwards to get a better understanding of a new condition that came to light after the urinary tract infections and the subsequent ultrasound and CT scans. It showed that I had cysts and a small stone in each kidney and a benign tumour in the right kidney. I also had cysts in the liver and small density on both lower lobes of my lungs. I was told not to worry about the lungs but further investigation was needed in regards to the other matters so I was referred first to a professor of renal medicine.

At first, I felt flabbergasted at what had shown up and indeed the professor confessed he had never seen so many things on one scan. He assured me that none of them required treatment and that all of these things are common in a large majority of people who, like me, are unaware until some further examination is called for. I felt relieved hearing this information though still a little shocked at what was going on inside my body.

Meanwhile understanding the correlation between mind and body I searched deep inside and felt great sadness and I wanted to nurture myself with unconditional love. I began to question who I was underneath my life experiences and at the core of my Being.

Subsequently I had a dream where I was told that I was meant to bring through spirits because I was a kind and gentle person. This amused me for two reasons: I can remember being afraid of ghosts and spirits from a very early age so I was quite intrigued by the dream and of course it may not mean the obvious as dreams rarely do.

I see writing as a form of bringing through spirits by sharing the information they have for us. Although I believe I can be kind and gentle it is not necessarily the impression I give others. I can be quite forceful in a 'tough love' kind of way. When I told my friend Amanda about my dream she laughed having been on the receiving end of my brusque exterior which is really a form of protection and self-preservation.

I can be quite stubborn, critical and bombastic but I knew that the dream reflected my true essence and I began to think about how life would be if I embodied this kind and gentle person. *I am still working on that one.*

The dream was a new beginning as I was really stuck in being the sort of *me* that I had created throughout the years. At times I was filled with frustration and feelings of mediocrity at my lack of success in my chosen fields. My concept of success was fairly rigid. In reality I had touched many lives in a positive way but I had preconceived ideas about what success was. I believed that to be a successful writer I had to be swept up by a large publishing company and sell millions of books. Ego had a large part to play in how I viewed life back then.

I somehow felt that my recent dream wasn't referring to the way I used to work but rather that it involved a new development that I was not yet fully aware of.

I had a fear of encountering spirits that came from childhood. I often know I am being visited and long to see them but fear prevents me from opening up completely. I am working on allowing myself to step forward in that regard. I am a very visual kind of learner so seeing is my first choice. I have seen clairvoyantly in the past but my real desire is to see my visitors the way I can see living people. Perhaps in my next book you will hear more about that!

As I said previously I had been frustrated with the small audience of my books as I self-publish and don't have funds left over for marketing and self-promotion. Besides which neither things sit well with me, even though I fully understand that it is the accepted way of producing successful books. But what constitutes success?

I want to be my unique self and not fall sway to the accepted way of doing things and if I am truly a creator then I know I can create in the way that was designed for me by me. I wanted to step outside of the box of accepted formulas and be myself. I became aware that I could really do this. Spirit enlightened me by telling me this. *'It isn't how many people read your books that matters. What matters is that those who do read them get maximum benefit from them therefore getting exactly what they need.'* That was a 'wow' moment for me and put things into perspective. I felt like I was touching the truth at last, rather than trying to conform to the stress of success and feeling uncomfortable.

Letting go of old ideas, concepts, issues, hurts and pain were highest on the agenda for my new emerging story. I didn't want to take the old adapted me into the future and with the insights that were coming I felt like I was going in the right direction. Even though I wasn't sure where I was going I felt excited. This is the adventure of working with spiritual matters; you never quite know where you will end up.

I became aware of so many things while dealing with the issues that had been uncovered and it gave me an opportunity to look at old emotional left overs and to let them go once and for all. What I didn't expect was an eruption like Vesuvius but it came fast and furious. I exploded in a fit of anger and frustration one Sunday when faced with the same old boring routine. I have lived with a consuming boredom and frustration for a long time. Every now and then I would have a mini eruption and move on not really having identified the underlying causes nor feeling any sense of having resolved anything. So on my meltdown day I started to look deeply inwards still fuming and physically feeling off. I began to unravel a core feeling of pure dislike of myself including my earlier life decisions. I had thoughts of not wanting to be incarnated in a physical body which surprised me as I have a very human concern about not being here.

The interesting thing was that a couple of nights before I had visualised dissolving the cysts in my liver and kidneys. The liver is the seat of anger so I believe my visualisation had somehow precipitated my outburst. The kidneys are filters that help to eliminate toxins through the urinary tract. As I had previously had recurrent urinary tract infections it was all starting to make sense. I needed to have this experience and these particular health challenges at this time in order to identify and release these deeply buried feelings.

I remembered a lovely gentle man that I had worked for many years ago. He had suffered from depression most of his life which I found astonishing as his outward appearance was of someone who had it all together, which of course is a common misconception. One day aged in his seventies he simply walked off the gap (a large cliff) in Sydney and plunged to his death. I could not imagine doing that because I am not brave enough. Then I realised that it wasn't bravery that gave him courage to do it, it was desperation. He was no longer able to live with his inner demon of depression.

Sometimes we are so caught in the net of illusion that nothing else seems real. The physical, mental and emotional components of life can be so convincing and overwhelming that we become trapped in the nightmare

Fortunately for me being aware of this helped me with

my own strong feelings of dislike. I knew that I must not run from mine. I had to face the demons within so that I could reconcile with them and move on.

These feelings had been buried for a long time and though I hated having them, I honoured the fact that they were there. I had been captive to them through unconscious behaviours and patterns. Luckily I am married to a strong and loving man who can bear my meltdowns even though he neither likes them nor understands them. Fortunately they are now much less frequent or necessary.

Once my understanding became clearer my energy was boosted and I didn't feel so weighed down. I knew that I still had work to do to unravel and heal this re-emerging story. If we fail to see and recognise things the body will find a way to speak to us in terms that demand our attention.

I fortuitously found a free one hour talk on how to heal through writing, hosted by *The Shift Network* featuring Mark Matousek. It appealed to me as a writer especially as it has always been easy for me to express myself through the written word. I knew that I had healing work to do and I had done a little journaling in the past but nothing serious.

Mark set out nine steps to this particular form of journaling and I decided I would follow the guidelines and see what happened. From the start I noticed a difference. I consciously and deliberately went to the edge of the pit of my unconscious and began to abseil into the abyss. Curiously it felt safe and I was eager to uncover the things that were preventing me from creating the life I wanted. I particularly wanted to discover my genius. So far I hadn't recognised what it could be because I didn't know I had any kind of genius. I was eager to see what might be revealed.

In seeking my truth I realised that it can take a lot of effort to uncover but the effort isn't in seeking the truth it is in the letting go of the false truths that we adopt as children.

Letting go sounds simple but can be profoundly difficult and is incremental. If we were able to move out of our old state into a completely new one immediately I am sure we would all do it. New states bring new energies along with much pleasanter and renewed enthusiasm for the journey that we are on.

Prising the old stuff loose sometimes requires the metaphysical equivalent of a jack hammer. We are creatures of habit and don't change easily or without resistance. This is how it is being human and there is nothing wrong in that. Our moral agendas often help us through difficult times, however they can also prevent us from knowing the deeper truths that are beyond moral judgements. Sometimes we are so consumed by our beliefs that we limit our view of life and its many layers. In expansion we can find greater truth and see the bigger picture. This expansion happens when the time is right and the pupil is ready.

Never let belief stand in the way of knowing, for one is acquired the other is inbuilt. Giving up struggle means that you can see more opportunities as they arise. You literally go with the flow: there is no resistance. Every opportunity gives you the chance to follow intuition and inner guidance or give in to the ego.

Sometimes it requires that you be brave enough to follow a lead without knowing where it will take you. It may be that initially it seems as if nothing is happening but seeds are being sown and the results will be evident a little later. At best, trusting the process will take you in a direction that you want to follow, at worst it becomes character building.

What may seem to be dead ends aren't personal failures, they are experiences to learn from and opportunities to hone your intuitive skills. I love this saying from a good friend of mine, 'If you keep banging your head on a closed door, don't be surprised when you get a headache'.

Sometimes I have had many a metaphysical bruise before noticing that the door wasn't opening. I believed I needed to knock louder to get a response. I guess there is a fine line between persistence and awareness that it isn't the right door.

Connie Howell

Become the author of your own life.
Don't let anyone else direct the pen
As the author you can create anything.
Imagination is a valuable tool of creation
Might as well let it go wild

If you knocked on the door
Rang the bell
Yelled and screamed
But still the door didn't open
Move on it isn't your door

Chapter 13

Layer upon Layer

I don't know if you ever saw the advertisements for Sara Lee strudels but the voice over said 'layer upon layer' when referring to the pastry. That little phrase has stuck in my head for years and is perfect for explaining the chakra make up and issues relating to them.

In my last book *Walking Between Two Worlds* I covered the basic anatomy of the chakra system but Spirit has been nudging me to go deeper. I am not an expert when it comes to knowledge about the chakras. I have some understanding of course, as I have trained in many kinds of healing that requires knowing about them, what they do and how they represent the different aspects of life.

They connect to nerve plexuses, endocrine glands and physiological and emotional aspects of life. I am now required to give a little more information that won't be new to some of you but may be helpful for beginners. So here goes.

We are multidimensional in nature. The chakras play a vital role in our overall health not just physically but also mentally, emotionally and spiritually. They connect us to the physical aspects of life and extend to us the ability to connect to the cosmos.

This connection gives us communication with higher consciousness, our Higher Self and the innate understanding of Universal laws. Through these portals we can create and manifest on a greater and grander level. The energies from the layers of the chakras surround us and envelop the human body energising, feeding and nourishing it. They are filled with information in the form of light, colour and energy. We literally buzz with activity especially when we are healthy in all aspects of mind, body and spirit.

Though I do not physically see the layers I can sense them in my deeper awareness and it is a beautiful dance of rainbow colours. I have on occasion seen partial layers around people and I can sense where there is a problem. Being a chakra reader is not my mission but I do find them fascinating and I have worked within the energetic field of others when I was a practitioner of energy healing, shamanic practices and as a massage therapist. That is because all of these practices require entering into the client's energetic imprint.

I can often sense things and hear telepathically. I can sometimes see clairvoyantly and can smell aromas and fragrances connected to other dimensions. The true meaning of the word clairvoyant is clear sight. These abilities came at first spontaneously then as a natural progression of opening up to higher dimensions and being dedicated to my spiritual unfoldment. In the beginning the abilities were exciting and somewhat unknown to me. With the passage of time I became more confident and trusting of them. They are also attributes of a healthy chakra system.

By knowing about and working with the layers of your chakras you can improve your health and wellbeing, as well as interacting with other dimensions. Past lives can be accessed along with knowledge that is beyond present understanding.

The more you use what you have the more that will be revealed. Most people that undertake a healing journey despair at the recurrence of old issues that seem to resurface over and again even when they have been dealt with previously. It is like peeling the layers off an onion, there always seems to be another layer underneath and sometimes it makes make you cry. The energy field around us connects body, mind and spirit. It directs, filters and assimilates energies into the body.

The chakras are multifaceted and each one has a colour, name and sound vibration plus an element. If a chakra's energy is distorted then the healthy vibrational energy cannot penetrate to full capacity and will need some kind of healing or clearing to bring it back to optimum capacity. Each colour and sound has its own vibrational energy.

Colour has a language of its own. What we wear and the colours we surround ourselves with can either uplift or depress our moods. Colour has a symbolic, spiritual, mental, emotional and energetic impact on our psyche. Culturally we have varying beliefs about the same colours. Some cultures believe that a certain colour may be lucky or unlucky. We have many symbolic references that are well known to us all. Most of us don't really give colour a conscious thought yet we know that by wearing a colour that suits us we feel better.

The seven best known chakra colours are red, orange, yellow, green, blue, indigo and violet. Red has the longest wavelength and slowest frequency. It is both grounding, and stimulating. It is connected to passion and the sex drive and all the earthy, basic emotions. It is also a thermal colour so makes us feel warm and cosy.

Orange strengthens the etheric body, is good for absorbing shocks and is also about deep joy. Yellow helps us to digest life and to connect to wisdom and to the intellect. It also relates to fear and the nervous system. It governs the digestive system.

Green is the balancer and space giver when we need to get away from it all and it helps us to create boundaries. It is a calming harmoniser but can also indicate envy. Green is mid-point in the chakra system and is sometimes referred to as the bridge between the lower and higher chakras. It relates to the heart and love.

Blue is a cool colour and peace bringer. Strongly connected with communications and expressing ourselves. It can be used to calm and bring peace but too much can indicate depression.

Indigo is the colour that helps inspiration and intuition. It connects with clairvoyance and mysticism. There is much to discover in the inky depths.

Violet is spiritually calming and can bring Heaven to Earth. It can also indicate hidden anger and grief. It relates to the top of head specifically the crown area.

For more information about colour see the suggested reading list at the back of the book. The body is intelligent and can deal with all kinds of conditions but when overloaded it may struggle to maintain or regain equilibrium. Nutrients will fail to be adequately delivered or taken up where needed and when muscles are tense, blood flow is impeded which allows toxins to build up.

There are many methods to cleanse and balance the chakras, some of which are sound therapy, chanting, various energy healing techniques and colour therapy. In some traditions each chakra has a corresponding chant associated with it.

So let's begin with the first three chakras. These connect us to the physical, emotional and mental aspects of life. They are relevant to survival, feelings and thoughts.

The first chakra which relates to the colour red and the element earth is called Muladhara which means root or support. Through this chakra we are connected to the earth which grounds us and gives us a firm foundation. The chant associated with it is LAM.

It is aptly named the root chakra and connects us to the feminine and to Mother Earth. Also the ages of nought to seven are related to this centre. In this chakra we are concerned with survival. The basic survival needs are food, shelter, safety and procreation.

If we don't feel connected to the earth we may flounder like a rudderless ship adrift on a choppy sea. It is especially important to be grounded when reaching into the higher dimensions but is also necessary to stay grounded when dealing with daily life.

The second chakra corresponds to the colour orange and the element of water. The earth element needs water to give it movement otherwise it may stagnate. This chakra has the name Svadhisthana which means sweetness and is said to be the dwelling place of the self. The chant is VAM. It covers the ages of eight to fourteen and digests emotional issues.

It is related to how we integrate relationships whether they are personal, sexual or professional. It is the home of passion and emotional boundaries. If negative experiences aren't digested and eliminated properly they will become inert and cause problems in the related areas. We also find the capacity for joy and laughter and the ability to have fun here.

The third chakra corresponds to the colour yellow and the element of fire, hence the name solar plexus. Solar refers to the sun and plexus innervates this area of our body. It has the chant RAM and it is called Manipura which means luscious gem. It relates to the ages of fourteen to twenty one.

The stomach is a hive of activity and if not innervated properly clear thinking and physical energy goes out the window. This is where our gut instincts can be adversely affected if this chakra is not in top working condition.

Often we are sensitive in this area to other energies that come from outside of us and if unbalanced we can feel low in energy and enthusiasm. It is also about personal power and we can feel courageous or fearful depending on our state of being. The fire element can direct energy but if it becomes overactive we can get digestive issues.

The fourth chakra is the heart chakra, the colour is green and the corresponding element is air. Its name is Anahata meaning unstuck and is chronologically associated with the ages of twenty one to twenty eight. The chant for this centre is YAM.

The heart chakra is where we feel love and compassion and we can let go of the desire for 'things' that give us status and importance. However, it is not necessarily the love of romance novels but the greater love of creation and selfless love. It is the bridge between the lower three physical chakras and the higher vibrational ones. In this chakra we can feel free of the need for material goods knowing that we always have what we need without ego.

The heart has its own wisdom and when balanced it can direct us to act with love and compassion. The air element can affect the breath and can either be harnessed or impeded. If you carry too much unexpressed grief for instance the air can be thwarted and affect the lungs and heart. Alternatively learning to focus on the breath is both meditative and calming bringing balance and harmony.

The fifth chakra is the throat centre and has the chant HAM. The colour is blue and the element is light, corresponding to the ages of twenty eight to thirty five and called Vishuda which means purification. This is our psychic centre where we have clairvoyance, clairaudience and clairsentient abilities. We also use this centre to speak our truth and communicate. If we hold back unable to speak up we may get throat or thyroid problems. This chakra influences how we metabolise food as it influences the thyroid, so body weight and temperature can be affected if we are not balanced here. If we don't feel spiritually, mentally or emotionally nourished we may not be able to metabolise these energies well either.

The sixth chakra is the third eye centre, the colour is indigo, (some say purple) the element is pure light and the chant is Om. It is called Ajna, meaning to know. Here we can shed the idea of a human being and realise that we are eternal but temporarily inhabiting a physical body. It is where we have insight. To be authentic one must shed the notion of being the personality and let go of the mental ideas that have been built preventing the realisation of the Divinity within ourselves and others. Doubts created by the mind interfere with knowing the truth, information becomes mistaken for knowledge. The mind loves information believing it to be superior, but knowing is a deeper truth that comes from the wisdom of the heart.

The seventh chakra is the pure energy and the colour violet and the chant for this one may vary between traditions so I am not going to state it. This chakra connects us to Heaven and goes by the name Sahasrara which means thousandfold. This is where we have undivided consciousness. We connect to the oneness, to awareness.

The first chakra grounds us and connects us to the earth, the second gives nourishment to the first. The third moves and directs the energy; the fourth connects us with the attributes of love, forgiveness and compassion. With the fifth we express our truth, the sixth gives us insight and the seventh chakra connects us to awareness without duality. It allows us to draw the pure light of the heavens down to nourish our complete chakra system whilst meeting the energies from the ground up. It is here that we can attain the mastery, over time, of breaking free from linear time to live only in the now. The sixth, seventh and eighth chakras are where development becomes transpersonal. They are supported by us being grounded in the physical so that we can reach up fully rooted and supported enabling us to integrate these higher qualities.

We are in physical bodies on purpose so we are not meant to try and escape into the spiritual dimensions at the expense of our physicality. We are to bring Heaven to Earth and reap the benefits of demonstrating all aspects of our Being. We can create from higher wisdoms beyond our personal egoic desires when we fully integrate all that we are.

All of the chakras may have imbalances at differing times and the negative side of the energy will be expressed either through the physical body or through the ego. Sometimes there may be too much energy and other times not enough. It is somewhat of a delicate balance and even when work has been done to clear oneself of the issues that influence each chakra we may find yet another layer to deal with. May I encourage you to keep peeling the layers because eventually you will get to the wonderful and delicious dessert you have so earnestly been seeking.

Some ways to work on bringing balance and clearing to the chakras are: chanting, sound therapy, aromatherapy, cleaning the chakras whilst in the shower, energy work, shamanic therapies, and breath work. Aura-Soma colour therapy works directly with the chakra system, and simply being out in nature can have a beneficial effect. Placing your bare feet on the grass or ground and swimming in the ocean or other bodies of water are grounding and cleansing too.

There is so much excellent information available about the chakra system and the luminous energy field through books, courses and the internet. All it takes is the interest to go find it.

Connie Howell

When all your chakras are balanced and in alignment
You become in harmony with the universe. You bring Heaven to
Earth
And dance the dance of the sacred.
You become like the rainbow
Full of colour and able to bring joy to those who see you

Chapter 14

Life is a journey

My journey this lifetime began on the 30th of May 1949 in a maternity hospital called Fern Lea. I was born in Lancashire, England. I was the last and totally unexpected pregnancy. I was preceded by three siblings, a brother being the eldest and two sisters. No doubt being the last child was an enormous relief to my mother who had suffered a tumultuous life whilst married to my father both physically and emotionally.

I am not sure at what age I began to shut down a little from life but feel that it was early on. It was neither a conscious decision nor a deliberate choice. Rather it was more likely a necessary component of dealing with a less than perfect life.

I loved going to school and the learning it provided me with, but as I grew a little older I had little ambition or drive. In fact I had no concept of achieving anything of any significance even though I was intelligent and had confidence.

Various situations that I found myself in began the slow erosion of that confidence and replaced it with a lack of self-worth and self-belief. I enjoyed learning new things as long as they captured my imagination but I lacked direction beyond my immediate future. My favourite subjects in senior school were English and history. My least favourite were maths, science and geography. In fact I hated science, couldn't fathom maths beyond a general level and geography seemed to confuse me.

However, I was generally thought of as someone who was clever and easy to get along with. My family saw me as intelligent with the ability to make friends easily. I had some good friends at school and got along with just about everyone. I can remember my mother teaching me the alphabet by singing it to me even before I began infant's school. I caught on quickly when the subject interested me and was taught in a fun way. We all have genius within us, whether we find it and accept is another matter. I never thought it possible for me to have any special ability because I always equated genius with outstanding academic and mental acumen beyond anything I could achieve.

Each of us is unique and allowing ourselves to be so rather than trying to fit in to the societal standards of excellence is a struggle most of us face at some time. Conformity is still alive and doing well.

It has taken me many years with a lot of struggling to learn to be myself displaying not only my better side but also the gnarly warts and all. I no longer engage with others at a superficial level. I fought hard with the concept of trying to be perfect and living up to what I thought people expected of me whilst silently experiencing much disquiet inside. This is not so true now. I am happily growing into *myself*.

As a teenager I began to numb and deny some of the more so called moral and socially unacceptable behaviours. I was sexually active with raging hormones and was enveloped by the swinging sixties. I did the sex and rock 'n' roll but never got into drugs other than cigarettes. Being from a family that struggled to make ends meet I had a period where

Lifting the Veil

I stole makeup and nylon stockings from the local Woolworths store but then I got caught.

When my mother found out she was so incensed she made me undress and stand naked in front of my step-father. She gave me a beating with a belt which was the usual form of punishment in our house when any of us did something considered really bad. I had felt humiliation before, but this was the worst time until I was in my thirties and once again experienced humiliation in a savage way.

In my late twenties and early thirties some of my emotional baggage around childhood spilled over into panic attacks and bouts of anxiety triggered by anything and everything. They began unexpectedly as I was due to leave home one day to pick up my youngest son from school. They lasted five years.

My story is not uncommon I see the same or similar scenarios in the lives of my friends and others that I meet and it causes them as much angst as it did me.

I grew up in an England that I loved and still do but I moved to Australia at the age of twenty-four with my three children, two suitcases and a hope for a better life. I came to be with an Australian man that I met in England and we married after four years when my partner finally was granted a divorce from his first wife. We have lived here since, but I am no longer married to that same man. Thank goodness—but that is another story.

The spiritual part of my journey began in Australia at the age of twenty-eight. I quite suddenly became aware of spirit beings and life after death. It occurred after my first ever visit to a spiritualist church. I had a lot of psychic phenomenon happen to me around that time and for several years thereafter. I decided to dig deeper and see if I could find out why I and everyone else is born. I was curious about why we live a certain amount of years then die. It was a question always in the back of my mind. I also wanted to know what the purpose of life actually was, because quite frankly I wondered at times.

It seemed odd to me that we are born only to die often with excruciatingly painful illnesses or disease. It just didn't make sense to me. At the time it was like the idea I had about teeth, it hurts like hell to get them, it can hurt like hell having them and some people have to get rid of all of them and have false ones. It seemed like a lot of unnecessary pain to me. What a lot of trouble to be subjected to. I figured there must be a better way. I guess that is how I viewed life back then. Life seemed to cause pain in such a lot of different ways.

I learnt over subsequent years and with the benefit of training in many forms of healing modalities that we are more than a physical body with a limited life expectancy. I found that what I considered to be reality was just one notion of reality and that there is so much more to be aware of. If you can find the key to opening your inner vision or if it spontaneously opens as mine did then things begin to make a little more sense. For me the timing was right; Divine timing that is.

I cannot stress strongly enough that there are many paths that lead to finding the truth and that truth itself is subjective depending on your life experience. Enlightenment has many stages. I believe the first stage is the awareness and exploration of other dimensions beyond this physical one. I am not talking about cosmic 'woo woo' stuff. I am referring to waking up from the collective dream and deep comatose state of living. In this physical world as a human being the idea of having no connection to the universe or other world beings is not my reality.

Though many believe in a greater Being that some call God, Source or Higher consciousness, the idea that we all have an intimate and unbreakable connection with it is an elusive if not an impossible concept. Direct revelation is not encouraged by members of some faiths.

The belief that there has to be an intermediary who acts on our behalf is prevalent, especially for those who see the rest of us as sinners that need to be saved. I am not condemning any other faith I am offering an alternative view and my own experiences. I have seen the dark and negative side of religion along with the good.

Intolerance is one of the most pervasive ills of life and creates barriers between all of us. It disallows intimate personal knowing and interactions. Acceptance by some and criticism from others permeates every area of our lives. Every time we feel intolerant towards another person of a different faith, race or belief we distance ourselves from love. Intolerance is a form of fear and arrogance.

By being intolerant we project the superiority of our own beliefs and judgements onto others. Our indignation and addiction to being right overrides reason as we hotly pursue and find ways to reinforce our way or the highway. The barriers between us become more solid and harder to break through. We look for reinforcements from others with the same views as our own to project outwards enabling the 'them and us' mentality to continue.

The more solid the energetic walls between us the more we isolate ourselves from each other and compassion is lost.

We find ways to construct bigger and stronger divisions to make the isolation complete. Society becomes at odds with itself, countries are alienated and power plays become destructive in the extreme. Hate spreads, fear ignites and voila: Pandora's Box is not only opened but the lid is nowhere to be seen in order to be put back on the box.

The way to bring down the wall is one brick at a time. If one person shows that vitriol and intolerance can be replaced with love, compassion and the willingness to be wrong then others can follow their lead and change nature into nurture. It can begin the process of making change at the core level. We are all energetically linked through the matrix of life and one by one we can refuse to be drawn into the illusion that there is only one way, one path to peace and cooperation.

We all contribute to the world with our thoughts and opinions. If you don't have inner peace you cannot contribute peace because you are at war with yourself. The outer world is a reflection of all our inner worlds. We are responsible for how the world is at any given moment and it is us as individuals and as a collective that need to fix it.

None of us have the whole truth, we each have fragments. What is true for one person may not be true for another. That is why there are many paths, many teachers and many experiences unique to every individual. Embrace the uniqueness of your own path without the need to judge or convert others and you will be a living example of compassion and tolerance.

When the mirror of illusion finally cracks the images previously held onto so tightly will dissolve into a million pieces, allowing us to reconstruct ourselves in a more

Lifting the Veil

wholesome and loving way. We are all in this together. We all have a part to play. We have similar thoughts and feelings no matter what language the mind hears them in. We have much more in common than we have differences. Our hearts all beat; our lungs breathe and our muscles allow movement. Cut us open and we all bleed red blood. These are the common bonds of being in a physical body.

We also have an innate need to connect with something deeper and more meaningful. We share common fears, desires and needs so how can we be separate when we are so alike? All of us are born from the universe and we rely on the earth for our existence. We are not separate except in our minds and the sooner we realise this the sooner we can get on and create a better world. A world in which we can thrive and live as equals is possible but would take a massive effort to achieve. A dream perhaps but we have dreamed the world into being as it is now so why not create a better dream?

Despite the ills, suffering and sacrifices that life asks of us there is an undeniable beauty if you allow yourself to see it. Walking with the sun shining lifts the spirits and for a moment or two you can get lost in the mystery of nature. By opening your heart as you walk with contemplation and awareness you can disengage from the outer world and find peace in the serenity and power of this gorgeous planet.

If you go even deeper you may even become open to other dimensions and see beyond the physical reality to connect with other wisdoms. This can be enriching to your overall life experience. Conversely walking on a winter's day with a chill in the air gives you a briskness that makes every pore seem alive. There are so many ways to switch off the constantly running commentary of bad news and tune into loving, nurturing energies.

Forgiveness of self and others is crucial if you want to progress in a positive way. Forgiveness doesn't mean accepting the unacceptable it means disengaging yourself emotionally from the chains of servitude to hate and revenge. This helps you more than anyone else and it makes you healthier and more compassionate and better able to understand the errors of judgement that everyone makes at some time or other.

Heinous crimes are difficult to forgive and I am not proposing that anyone overlook atrocities but we can either become stuck in the mud and mire of it or we can free ourselves of the junk so that we can make a difference where it counts. We can become a force for love rather than perpetuating hate.

To step outside of the whirl of emotional debris and find peace amidst chaos is no easy feat and by no means have I fully succeeded. By taking time out to connect with the beauty of life itself I can disentangle myself more often and catch my breath to inhale some goodness and carry on.

Peace is a word easily bandied about and most of us purport to wanting it, especially world peace, and yet we are at war with ourselves and each other day in and day out. It must be understood that world peace starts with each of us finding the peace within ourselves and our own lives. We need to stop contributing to the outpouring of anger and projections of hate. Posturing and power struggles are so prevalent and evident today.

There is fear and concern amongst us that is hard to dispel but if we do not try we are guilty of adding to the woes and dramas that are being acted out every day. If we think and believe that we can do nothing then nothing changes. Making a difference doesn't have to be a highly visible thing, just spending time each day on self-examination and the conscious promotion of love from the self to others is a powerful contribution to the outcome of world events. Feeling powerless plays directly into the hands of those whose desires are less than honourable and who like to promote the idea that violence is the only way to overcome adversaries. Violence simply creates more violence, more fear and more victimology.

When we hold on to our belief that there is only one way or one ideal method to attain mysticism or spirituality we automatically negate all other views and experiences. We do this in order to remain right!

This is both ludicrous and self-righteous. There are many ways, ideals and paths that will get you to enlightenment. It will come to everyone eventually. No road is the only road and there isn't one faith or belief that is the only way. The universe speaks to us all individually, after all we are made to be unique, so we must respond accordingly.

Let's not be arrogant, stubbornly refusing to accept that others may feel differently than we do as to how they answer the call of their soul. We don't have to make them wrong just so we can feel superior believing we have found the way but that they have not. Just because it may not fit with our own belief does not make it wrong. Of course, we don't have to agree but we would all benefit if we simply allow rather than use tactics that try to coerce, bully or scare.

Through humility we are able to travel our own route and let others travel theirs and often the result is that we all meet up in the end, regardless of the road we travel. It is great to have passion and faith especially if it comes through the heart, not the head. Sometimes listening to the passion of others can lead us to learn something new even if it is just that it strengthens our own experiences.

My life story began to change when I was going through my second divorce. I was given a simple affirmation by a friend. It was these four words *I deserve the best*. We all deserve the best but yet feeling inadequate and unworthy prevents the goodness coming to us. Self-doubt, eroded confidence and loss of power are all stumbling blocks—but they are not insurmountable.

You can change that story, rewrite it with flair and excellence then set about allowing it to manifest. It may take time, it may take effort but if you don't do it then who will?

Though there may be things in life that we cannot change we do have the power to change the way we think and react. In fact over time we can learn to respond rather that react and this in itself is a powerful adversary.

Taking little steps still moves you forward and if you fall don't be discouraged just live in the moment and know that with a little rest and the will to continue you will make progress.

I can't tell you how many times I have stopped and started again. Sometimes I was convinced I couldn't take one more step and at times I was totally disenchanted and lacked the will or the interest to keep moving but always some deeper part of myself motivated me to try again.

I have dissolved into hissy fits when life hasn't gone the way I think it should or if something is taking longer than my miniscule ability to be patient can bear. Yet the Universe keeps on loving me and supporting me—now that is unconditional love!

We so often get caught up in the reaching of destinations that we forget to enjoy the journey. It is especially hard to revel in the mysteries as we travel through life when there is hardship and trauma and it may seem that there is no joy in living. We have long forgotten why we came or that we agreed to come to enrich the growth of our soul.

When I let my mind settle on all the tragedies in the world such as starvation, poverty, war and all kinds of abuse and cruelty I can see how extremely difficult it is for those directly affected. To face another day when that brings more of the same, takes immense courage. I am in awe of the human fortitude that it takes to survive against all odds.

The more of us that awaken to our true nature, finding within us the compassion and love so desperately needed in the world, the more we can make a difference. The so called 'reality' that we find ourselves in can be changed but we must believe that it is possible and then do what we can to help bring about a better future.

Once we quell our inner demons and fears we are free to step away from the automatic ways of reacting and we can step into the role of co-creators with confidence.

May your journey through life be more peaceful, loving and filled with joyous moments each and every day. Become contagious and spread your love and the light of your soul to all you meet. For me, life is a mystery that I may never truly understand but then I have always loved a good mystery.

Namaste

Connie Howell

May your journey be filled with the joy of adventure
Be your own tour guide
Plan your own route and destinations
Be your own travel agent and
Travel with the people you choose to be with
Go to places only dreamed of and bring them into reality
When you do that you show me that it can be done and
That anything is possible

Suggested Reading

Grow Up Your Ego, Ten Scientifically Validated Stages to Emotional and Spiritual Maturity.
   Gagan, Jeanette M. PhD
   Rio Chama Publications. 2013

The Hidden Messages in Water
   Masuro, Emoto

The Ecstasy of Surrender, 12 Surprising Ways Letting Go Can Empower Your Life.
   Orloff, Judith MD
   Harmony Books 2014

The Miracle of Colour Healing.
   Wall, Vicky
   The Aquarian Press 1990

Victim of Thought: Seeing the Illusion of Anxiety.
   Whalen, Jill 2017

Useful websites

http://www.conniehowell.com/
Information about the author

http://www.theshiftnetwork.com/
This is where you will find free online seminars by exceptional speakers

http://www.aura-soma.com/
Colour therapy courses and information

http://www.indiemosh.com/
Self-publishing packages and information

http://www.themoshshop.com.au/
Online book sales in Australia of books published by indiemosh including books by this author

http://www.myproofreader.com.au/
Proofreading and copyediting